the embroiderer's floral

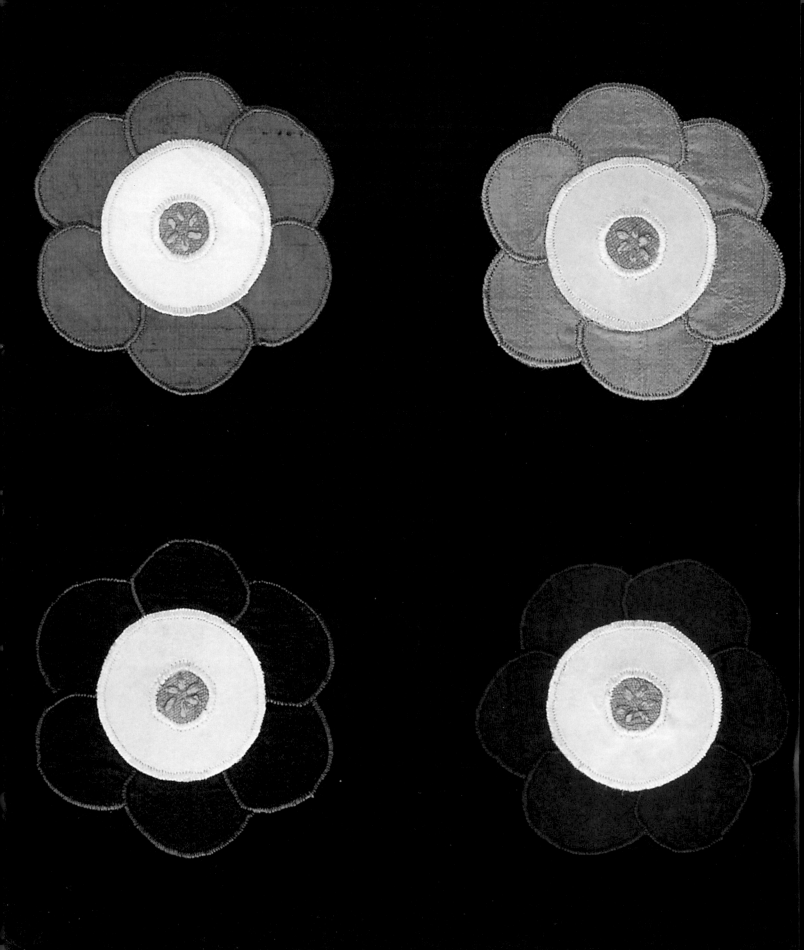

the embroiderer's floral

designs, stitches & motifs for popular flowers in embroidery

janet haigh

Photography by John Heseltine

KRAUSE

Published by Krause Publications

700 East State Street, Iola WI 54990-0001

www.krause.com

1 3 5 7 9 8 6 4 2

Library of Congress Cataloging-in-Publication Data

2002107615

ISBN 0-87349-443-1

Created and edited by Susan Berry

Designed by Debbie Mole

Illustrations by Janet Haigh *and* Coral Mula

Reproduction by Classic Scan, Singapore

Printed in Hong Kong

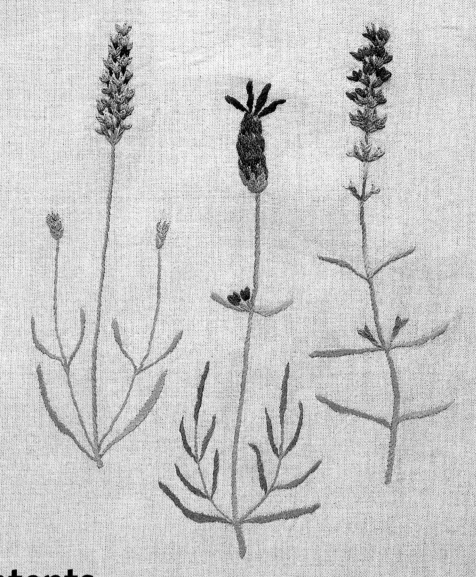

contents

INTRODUCTION

above: heart memento

This commission was for a first wedding anniversary gift. It is embroidered with the couple's initials, the date and a copy of their wedding bouquet of lilies and deep red roses.

I HAVE BEEN DRAWING and embroidering flowers all my life. As a child, my mother taught me "lazy daisy" stitch along with the other basic sewing skills that all girls were expected to develop in those days. As an art student, I embellished my clothes with all kinds of floral motifs during the "flower power" days of the '60s.

When I moved to London to work as a fashion designer, I drew flower-embroidered motifs to be appliquéd onto the dresses I designed, but, more tellingly, I also embroidered pictures, for myself, of imaginary gardens filled with flowers, as I lived without a garden.

Those early embroideries were fantasies, fuelled by studying garden design books and later by visits to the seasonal flower shows held throughout Britain, where the most beautiful specimens win prizes and the newest plants are displayed. I became fascinated by the whole world of flowers and gardens. By the time that I acquired a garden of my own, I was exhibiting my garden embroideries and starting to earn my living as a designer of all different types of hand embroidery, which somehow or other always seemed to include flowers.

Flowers and embroidery are inextricably linked in the English language. In the past the verb "to flower" was a synonym for embroidery, and embroidered flowers are found recorded throughout textile history from ancient China to modern times. I think that most embroiderers are, at some point, motivated by the allure of flowers. They wish either to record them faithfully, as I have, or to discover ways to challenge the traditional techniques and express new ideas provoked by an evolving view of nature.

For me, the sheer beauty and fragility of flowers, and the colours, shapes and variations of individual species, make them fascinating to work. There is also a poignancy about flowers, as they last for such a short time and are seen in many cultures as symbols of our own transience.

Flowers are still important symbols in our everyday lives and I think that this is why I am continually drawn to using them in all aspects of my work. They are given as prizes along with the medals at sports' ceremonies, echoing the crowns of flowers given to both poets and heroes in the ancient world, as "thank you" gifts and as tokens to

6

above: wind flowers

In antiquity it was thought that anemones (or wind flowers) flowered only when the winds blew. My machine-embroidered appliqué depicts all kinds of anemone flowers being blown by the zephyr.

celebrate birthdays and wedding anniversaries, at least in our house. Red roses (a universal symbol of love) are given by lovers to mark St Valentine's Day. Brides wear head-dresses and carry armfuls of flowers, often white lilies – a symbol of purity and attributed to the Virgin Mary. In Western society, we take flowers when visiting the sick, probably to cheer them by bringing fresh, colourful life into their closed rooms. Finally, we offer them as tributes to the dead, either in the shape of funeral wreaths or as red poppies, the symbol of those fallen in battle, at war memorials.

As I became increasingly fascinated by flowers I started to study their history and learn about their symbolism. I read the Greek and Roman myths, where people who offended the gods could be turned into flowering plants, as was the youth Narcissus who fell in love with his own reflection. The ancient writers also explained the reasons for the names given to many flowers. Pliny records that anemones are also known as "wind flowers" since they were only to be found growing in windy conditions. I discovered that the ancient Turkish custom of giving flowers meanings was resurrected in the 19th century as the "language of flowers" and was used to send secret messages from friend to friend or lover to lover. The flower language is very curious to "read" now but has a certain charm that can still be used for sending simple messages. It proved a very amusing and decorative way of giving coded information about people who had commissioned

above and opposite: embroidered garden

This large commission for an embroidery of the garden at Burton Agnes Hall in Yorkshire, England (opposite) has a wealth of flowers with many cottage-garden favourites, such as delphiniums and poppies (above).

me to embroider their portraits, usually with their families or pets and often in their gardens.

How to embroider flowers to look real, as if they have just fallen onto the fabric, is something that I have tried to master for years. My admiration for Oriental silk embroidered flowers led me to research the techniques that they entail, to the extent of visiting Japan and studying its textiles. I realized that flowers featured on many kimonos. These exquisite silk embroideries inspired me to really refine my stitching skills as well as to study the way that plants grow and develop, so that design ideas flow from the qualities of the flower itself.

Most of the flowers featured in the book are developed from my work as a fashion textile designer. I designed embroidered fabric samples that were bought by fashion designers as inspiration for designing clothes. These repeating flower designs or motifs had to be made simply and be full of character – romantic roses, blowsy poppies and pert pinks. They also had to employ fashion fabrics, such as coloured velvets, silks, tweeds and tartans, rather than the neutral linens and cottons typical of traditional embroidery grounds. The ability to capture the character of a flower by studying its growing habits, together with the use of different fabrics and colours to accentuate this, is a crucial factor in achieving lively embroideries.

When designing flowers for embroidery there are several important things to consider. Firstly, the shape of the flower: is it round like a daisy, cup-shaped like a tulip or trumpeted like a daffodil? These shapes may lend an element of character that needs to be enhanced: the upright cup of the tulip is completely different in character from the simple, circular daisy: the former has elegance, the latter has charm. In fact, it would be difficult to make any daisy flowers appear elegant or sophisticated. These characteristics will affect your design, so it is useful to have an appreciation of them before choosing which flowers to select for a particular purpose.

The second consideration is the rhythm or habit of growth of a particular plant. Does it meander like climbing sweet peas, stand erect like alliums or elegantly droop like fritillaries? Again, try to define the over-riding characteristic and use this to your advantage: a twining plant is the natural choice for a border, for example. The colour is the next thing to consider: is it bright and bold like anemones, subtle and shadowy like hellebores, fresh like the daffodil or faded like late-season hydrangeas? Then consider which fabrics and threads will underline these effects. Strong colour requires solid silks that

for
Susan Cunliffe-Lister
to Record and Celebrate
Her New Elizabethan
Gardens at Burton Agnes
29 June 1995

IL TEMPO PASSA

Janet Haigh–Her Work
1995–96 • DJC • HLJ

opposite: auricula theatre

This embroidery was inspired by traditional auricula primrose theatres, where the flowers were displayed in a curtained enclosure that protected them.

hold the most intense dye or satins that reflect light. Subtle colours can be achieved through layers of transparent fabrics and threads that are space dyed through a range of shades: the overlap of colours always gives subtlety to a thread. Texture is often overlooked: consider whether it is velvety like a rose, crinkled like a poppy or silky like a lily.

Finally, consider the scale, not so much of the real flower but of the embroidery as a whole: does the flower have enough detail to be of interest when made really big and is the silhouette strong enough for a simplified, large treatment? Also, just how small can you make the embroidery so that all the necessary details are still apparent and easily stitched. The purpose of the following pages is to introduce my own ways of embroidering and designing with flowers. I have included a small range of techniques that should enable you to develop your own ideas, using either the motifs in the book or those of your own. The fabrics, ribbons and threads that I use are laid out for you to see, as are the rudiments of basic design in the chapter on Creating Floral Embroideries. These will enable you to develop flowers into all kinds of decorated textiles or stitch them with affection as presents.

One of the most informative aspects of this book is the tiny embroidery of the growing plant placed next to each flower name in the Floral Directory. These are the smallest and simplest ways that I have evolved to embroider plants as seen in a garden; they rely on studying the habit of growth and the colour of the whole plant when seen from a distance, so that you can create small embroidered portraits of your favourite flowers or flower groups from your own garden.

I hope that you enjoy studying the flower embroideries in this book as much as I have enjoyed making them and that you will gain inspiration, whether as a novice or experienced embroiderer, from their range and diversity, in form and colour as well as stitching techniques.

below: garden of eden

In this embroidery of mine, I have given the flowers an allegorical meaning: heaven is represented by a bowl of golden roses, hell by an insectivorous plant.

1 1

EQUIPMENT AND MATERIALS

WHEN STARTING to embroider flowers you will need both the threads and the materials to do so as well as the usual embroidery equipment. The embroideries in this book are both machine embroidered and hand embroidered. The machine embroideries do not use complicated stitches so you need only have a sewing machine that has a swing-needle facility.

equipment

You need both designing equipment and sewing equipment. For designing you will need: papers, such as graph, tracing, layout and drawing; pencils; paper scissors; eraser; rulers and set square. For sewing you will need: needles of various kinds, depending on thickness of yarn, scissors, thimble, tape measure, hoops and stretchers, pins, water-soluble pens and dressmaker's carbon.

embroidery threads

There is a wide selection of embroidery threads that are specially spun for machine or hand use. The threads can be natural for hand embroidery: silk, cotton or wool; or synthetic or natural for machine embroidery: silk or cotton for natural fabrics, viscose and rayon for synthetic ones.

hand-embroidery threads

The most commonly used embroidery thread is stranded cotton (embroidery floss), generally with six strands in each thread. These are the most versatile of all threads. You can work the stitches in various thicknesses, depending on the number of strands used. In addition to stranded cotton you can buy stranded silk, which comes in varying weights, with up to 12 strands per thread; it gives the embroidery a subtle lustre.

A twisted cotton thread, known as cotton perle (or pearl cotton), is a highly lustrous yarn perfect for decorative surface stitches. It comes in various weights, from the thickest, which is No 3, to the finest, which is No 12. No 5 is the most useful.

There are three main weights of wool yarn used in this book. Tapestry yarn, the thickest, is a 4-ply yarn, and is readily available. Crewel wool yarn is a 2-ply yarn and comes in two thicknesses; it can be used in single strands or in multiples.

colours

Most of the yarns and threads come in a wide range of colours and are graded into numerous shades of one colour. Crewel wool yarns, for example, come in sets of five or six shades of each colour. You can also buy space-dyed threads in silks, cottons and wools, in which myriad hues are blended in one skein. They give great subtlety to stitching.

machine-embroidery threads

The synthetic machine-embroidery threads are fine and silky. They are used for working on silk and other lustrous materials; they come in a wide range of colours, including shaded and multi-coloured versions. The regular cotton sewing-machine threads, which are widely available, come in an extensive range of shades. As they are slightly thicker than standard machine-embroidery threads, they are useful for appliqué: you can experiment with heavier than usual threads using the technique on page 22.

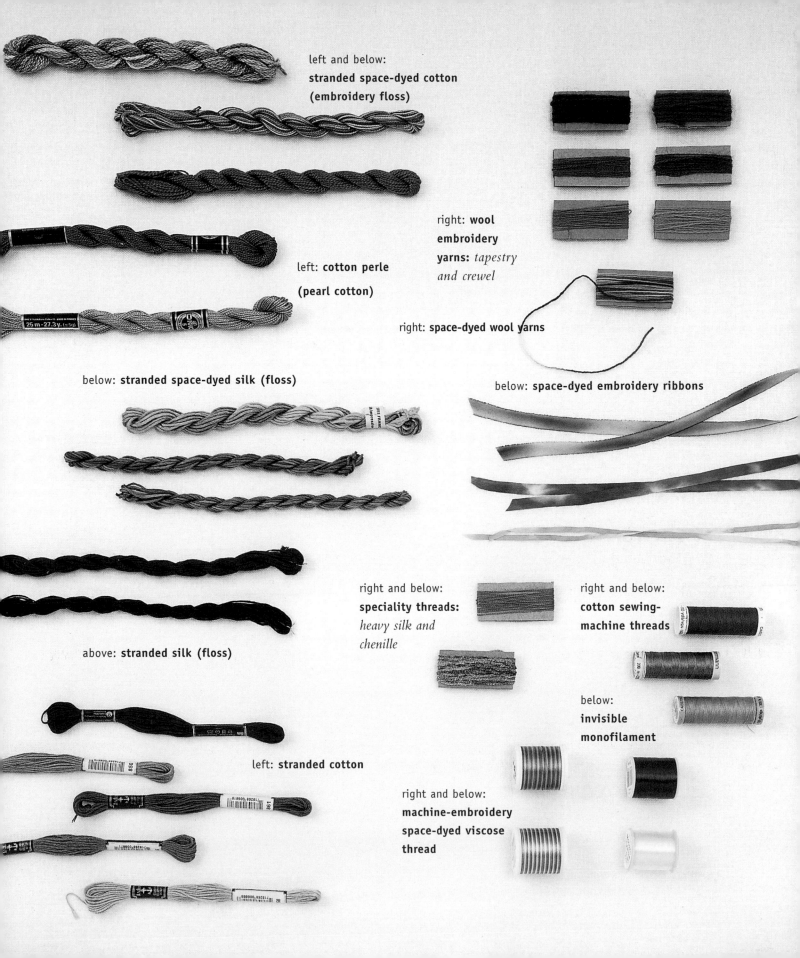

left and below:
**stranded space-dyed cotton
(embroidery floss)**

right: **wool
embroidery
yarns:** *tapestry
and crewel*

left: **cotton perle
(pearl cotton)**

right: **space-dyed wool yarns**

below: **stranded space-dyed silk (floss)**

below: **space-dyed embroidery ribbons**

right and below:
speciality threads:
*heavy silk and
chenille*

right and below:
**cotton sewing-
machine threads**

below:
**invisible
monofilament**

above: **stranded silk (floss)**

left: **stranded cotton**

right and below:
**machine-embroidery
space-dyed viscose
thread**

left and below: **coloured ribbons**

These include tartan, velvet, grosgrain, space-dyed and shaded types.

above right: **waste canvas**

Used for embroidering cross-stitch designs on any fabric.

right: **Aida braid**

This evenweave cross-stitch fabric comes in a range of widths and weights, some with edging details.

below: **neutral grounds**

These natural fibres – linen, cotton and silk – come in varying weights.

right: **coloured silks**

These are useful both as embroidery grounds and for appliqué.

materials

These include fabrics in various weaves, fibres, weights and colours, special fusible bonding materials and ribbons.

fabrics and bonding materials

You will need, first and foremost, a suitable ground fabric on which to embroider. For the purpose of clarity, the major embroideries in the Floral Directory are stitched on neutral grounds. These vary in weight and type, if not colour. Some are silks, some cottons, some linens, in varying weights and thicknesses.

In addition to natural colours, you can use richly coloured silk or cotton grounds. Coloured silks give real vibrancy to flower embroideries and are a good choice for appliqués. You can experiment with different weights, including silk organzas or coloured voiles for scarves or curtains, and heavy velvets for a much richer effect. Silk dupion is a fabric that I use a great deal, as it is excellent for appliqués. You can use any weight, but an iron-on backing will help to stabilize the fabric.

There are special fabrics for counted-thread embroideries, such as cross stitch. These are generally evenweave, linen or cotton fabrics that are graded in terms of the number of threads per inch or centimetre. Those with the highest thread count will produce embroideries with finer stitches. Aida is a popular evenweave cotton which comes in different forms and thicknesses. As it is dense, it is suitable for tablecloths, blinds and lightweight cushions. It is sold both as fabrics by the metre (yard) and as braids, woven to different widths, some with scalloped or contrasting borders, which are ideal for use as edgings.

In addition, there is a special fabric known as waste canvas. It is a starched evenweave fabric that can be placed on any non-counted-thread fabric as a guide for cross stitch. When it is dampened, after the embroidery is completed, the threads can be removed leaving the embroidered stitches in place on the ground fabric beneath it.

There are also special adhesive-treated fabrics for making fine embroidered fabrics strong enough to be stretched and worked. They come in varying weights, from very lightweight spun fibres with a film of heat-reactive adhesive sprayed on them (for fine silks) to heavier woven cottons sprayed with a granular heat-reactive adhesive. They come in either black or white. There is also a special paper, treated with adhesive, known as fusible web, which can be used to bond any two fabrics together.

ribbons

In addition to ground fabrics, you can purchase ribbons in many widths, which can also be used for appliqué work. Fine ribbons can be used like embroidery thread. The range of ribbon types is enormous: they can be found in many widths and weights.

Wide velvet ribbon is wonderful for rich appliqué work and is a less expensive option than buying velvet by the metre (yard) for small embroideries. Cotton grosgrain ribbon can also be used. Space-dyed ribbons, known as multi-hued or ombré, are featured in many of the embroideries. They come in a wide range of colours and widths.

Striped or checked ribbon, narrow or wide, can often add an attractive finishing touch to an embroidery: from a bow to a posy, for example.

15

creating floral embroideries

The following pages give the basic information on designing and techniques for all the flowers pictured in the book. Many of the techniques may be familiar to you already, as they are all simple and straightforward; they are included because they are my tried and trusted ways of working as an embroidery designer. The techniques include basics, such as tracing and enlarging a motif, as well as those techniques I frequently employ, such as machine embroidery, either for simple appliqués or for free-motion machine methods, crewel work and hand-embroidered lines and fillings. The design pages contain inspirational ideas on how to use embroidered flowers in many different ways, from mounting a small embroidery to making a precious picture or creating borders for a colourful cushion; how to repeat motifs to form a larger piece of fabric, such as a tablecloth or even curtains; and how to develop a whole embroidered border of garden flowers. To conclude, the section offers a gallery of simple projects using these design concepts and the flowers from the directory.

TRANSFERRING AND ENLARGING

MANY OF THE FLOWERS in the directory can be copied directly from the pages straight onto the fabric to be embroidered: the tracing methods are best for this. For more complicated techniques where several stages of construction are needed, the motif section on pages 140-155 provides all the separate pattern pieces and the drawings needed for the enlarged flowers.

To transfer the images of the flowers onto the ground fabric you will need tracing paper and a pencil, and a water-soluble pen for marking the traced design on the ground fabric. If your design requires a larger or smaller flower than that shown in the motif section, the simplest method is to use an enlarging or reducing photocopier and then trace the appropriately sized image from the copy. However, before copiers were invented, the traditional enlarging method was to use a grid (see opposite). When enlarging a motif for an appliqué, you need to trace a thin line along the outermost edge of the motif. For an embroidery motif, the varying widths of the outline must be recorded; if traced carefully, they will give a lively line to the simplest embroideries.

18

transferring designs

YOU WILL NEED a piece of dressmaker's carbon paper and/or tracing paper (depending on the method chosen), a sharp pencil and some masking tape. When making the initial tracing of the image to be transferred, either draw a fine pencil line on each side of the enlarged line or fill in between the line to make one solid outline so that you copy the outline exactly.

Method 1 *Place the fabric on a hard surface. Then pin the tracing to a piece of dressmaker's carbon paper, place the motif on the fabric and trace over the drawing using a very sharp pencil.*

Method 2 *If the fabric is light in colour and/or lightweight, secure the tracing to a window with masking tape, place your fabric on top of it and draw the motif using a water-soluble pen.*

superimposing designs

WHERE YOU ARE MAKING a more complex pattern, such as for a border, or one composed of individual groups of flowers, you may need to superimpose individual tracings to create the combined effect you are trying to achieve. This system is useful for making small posies of flowers as well, such as those on page 39.

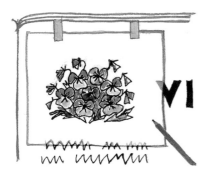

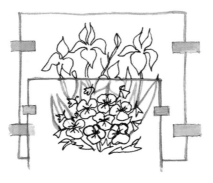

1 *Make tracings of the flowers from the motif section on transparent paper. It is important at this stage to check the comparative scale of the flowers and make any necessary alterations – the hydrangea bush is tiny when compared to the pink, for example.*

2 *Placing one drawing over another, make a decision as to which group should go in front (the smaller ground-hugging plants work best), then move the top tracing to create a balanced group; it may be necessary to adjust the motifs or add another group of flowers.*

3 *When the picture looks balanced, tape the tracings together; then trace the final combined design drawing so it is ready to be transferred onto the ground fabric. Trace this onto the fabric using a water-soluble pen.*

19

enlarging designs

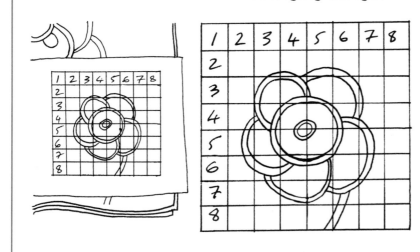

THE TRADITIONAL METHOD of enlarging is to mark the design in a grid, which then allows you to make a faithful larger duplicate. *Draw a grid over the initial tracing, with squares of 1cm ($^1/_2$in) (far left). Then calculate the ratio of the size that you want and draw the larger grid on another sheet of paper and transfer, square by square, the lines of the drawing (left). You may need to refine the drawing.*

EMBROIDERED LINES

ELEGANT EMBROIDERIES can easily be made by stitching over a simple line drawing. This is particularly suited to describing climbing plants, such as convolvulus or sweet peas with their twining tendrils, but any flower that has an interesting petal shape or a strong silhouette will work well. The first thing to consider is the choice and colour of thread. There are many interesting space-dyed threads that are perfect for capturing the nuance of colour found in flowers, and they come in many different weights and textures suitable for use by either hand or machine.

HAND-EMBROIDERED LINES

MY FAVOURITE stitches for line embroidery are stem and split stitch, which are ideal for slender curving stems. Very fine lines can be created using a single couched thread, while buttonhole stitch is an excellent outlining stitch for more graphic images, using heavier than usual threads.

split stitch

Nothing else quite gives the degree of control that enables you to pinpoint the spot to make your next stitch so that it will suggest a twist in a stem or to turn the tip of a leaf. The finest lines can be made using a single strand of stranded cotton (floss) for leaf veins, petal outlines and even some of the larger stamens. In heavier threads it can look like a tiny chain stitch and can be used in gradated colour to suggest a rounded stem.

stem stitch

For heavier or raised lines, it is easy to use stem stitches over a base of straight stitches to form a trammed line. This creates a subtle, three-dimensional effect. Slanting the stitches gives a fluid look to a delicately curved stem. On wider stems and stalks, outline the base stitches first and make sure that the stem stitches cover the outline without going beyond it, to give a neat edge.

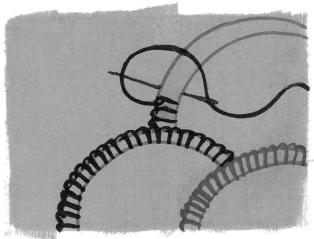

couched thread stitch

The thinnest line of all is the couched thread. If the finer thread is stitched in the same direction as the twist of the thread being couched down, then a continuous and sensuous fine raised line can be made, perfect for describing stamens, tendrils or stems on miniature embroideries. The embroideries on page 64, for example, make use of these particularly fine couched lines.

buttonhole stitch

Wide, bold lines that are both textured and hardwearing can be produced by buttonhole stitch; many old-fashioned flower embroideries on tray cloths, tablecloths and napkins can still be found adorned with these charming and naive line embroideries. Careful choice of thread will give controlled stitches: tightly plied and glossy pearl cotton, which comes in several thicknesses, is perfect for this type of work.

21

threads for heavier lines

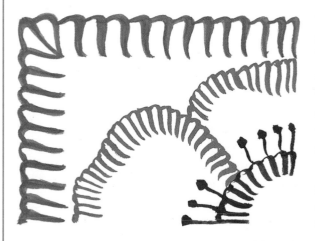

WHEN A VERY LARGE FLOWER is required for immediate impact not just the size of the flower is important but the techniques used must be considered carefully, as should the materials. Just as you need to consider the size of the drawn line when enlarging motifs, you also need to think about the scale of the threads that you will be embroidering with, whether by hand or machine.

The buttonhole-stitched flower on the linen napkin on page 59 faithfully follows the undulating petal outline to add vibrancy to a simple design. The embroidery is worked in a correspondingly thick pearl-cotton thread.

MACHINE-EMBROIDERED LINES

FOR MANY EMBROIDERIES, machine-embroidered lines are ideal, since they enable you to describe long flowing lines quickly and easily. Although fine thread is most often used for machine-stitched lines, you can, in fact, use heavier thread if needed, by employing the technique shown below right. A more modern method is to use free-motion machine stitching, which produces a "scribbled" pattern of randomly stitched lines. To work this you will need to keep the ground fabric stretched taut with an embroidery hoop (see opposite).

fine lines

FOR REALLY REFINED LINES that give lightness and freedom to stitched flowers and which are perfect for fine stems and tendrils, straight stitch can be used.

heavy lines

THICK THREADS can be wound onto the bobbin rather than needle-threaded. The embroidery is then worked with the fabric face-down on the machine.

This method is easier to work over a guideline drawn in water-soluble pen. It is best used in conjunction with embroidered appliqué, as simple machine-embroidered lines are very effective for linking up areas of appliqué. If a stem is to be described, several lines may be needed so it is worth experimenting with different thicknesses and types of thread — even those not intended for machine embroidery can be tried. Although the resulting embroideries are sparse, they are perfect for describing delicate flowers.

First trace the motif onto a piece of fusible interlining and press in position on the back of the work. (Remember that the motif will be reversed on the right side of the fabric, so reverse the drawing after tracing it.) Wind the thick yarn onto the bobbin (by hand if necessary) and loosen the tension screw until the yarn pulls freely through the bobbin clasp. Thread the needle with a neutral cotton and use maximum stitch size. Bring the bobbin thread through to the surface. Place the fabric face-side down and stitch over drawing using a straight stitch.

FREE-MOTION MACHINE LINES

FREE-MOTION MACHINE STITCHING can be used for embroidery but I most often use it on appliqué, although not primarily to apply one fabric to another, as using fusible web on fine fabrics does this job quickly and effectively. Free-motion machine stitching is useful to both strengthen the fabric bond and the design by describing the details of the flowers, especially if they are delicate. (In effect free-machined appliqués are machine embroideries on bonded motifs.) Use straight stitch for a fine line, zigzag stitch for wide ones.

23

1 *Remove the presser foot and its attachment from the machine. Stretch the fabric to be embroidered, right side uppermost, in a hoop so that the fabric will sit flush with the machine bed. The hoop keeps the tension on the fabric, but must be small enough to enable you to manipulate it without hitting the column of the machine, and large enough to give you room to complete enough of the embroidery at one time (the embroidery may need to be stitched in sections). Place the hoop under the needle and lower the presser foot. Then lower the needle into the fabric to bring the bobbin thread through to the surface of the embroidery.*

2 *Keeping the fabric close to the bed of the machine, move the hoop so that the needle stitches where you move, using either straight or zigzag stitch. Although this is like rubbing your stomach and patting your head at the same time, you quickly become used to manoeuvring the hoop. You may need to stitch a line at least twice when using fine machine embroidery threads so that any poor bits of sewing can be hidden next time around. The use of multi-coloured threads avoids changing threads: usually only a couple of colour changes are needed for a flower embroidery: a green blend for stems/leaves and one or two blends for flowers.*

EMBROIDERED FILLINGS

HOW TO EMBROIDER FLOWERS to look real, as if they have just fallen onto the fabric, is something that I have tried to master for years. Admiring the exquisite Oriental embroidered silk flowers made me research their methods, only to discover that they use exactly the same stitches and techniques that we do – mostly long and short stitch, and stem stitch with various knots – but with an expertise developed over centuries using the finest coloured, lustrous silk threads. Observation of the growing flower is important in order to understand how to position the threads so that they blend in a natural way, one colour giving way to another without the thread change showing.

If you do not draw well, or have just started embroidery, cross stitch, in which the stitches are uniformly created on a counted-thread ground, is one of the easiest techniques to master. There is a wide range of designs available for this ever-popular form of embroidery.

waste canvas cross-stitch technique

ALTHOUGH MOST PEOPLE assume you need an evenweave canvas on which you can count the threads to create a cross-stitch embroidery, you can, in fact, use plain weave ground fabrics if you employ the waste canvas technique shown here. This is particularly useful if you want to make a cross-stitch flower on, say, the pocket of a plain cotton dress. You can buy the waste canvas in different gauges of thread, just as you can evenweave fabrics.

1 *Cut a piece of waste canvas about 2.5cm (1in) larger than the motif and pin and baste the canvas in position on the ground fabric. Using a pointed needle, and following the chart provided, stitch through both the canvas and the fabric beneath.*

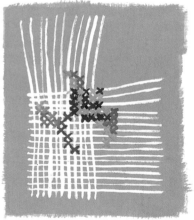

2 *When the motif is complete, trim away the canvas close to the embroidery. Dampen the remaining canvas threads and pull them out one by one until they have all been removed.*

designing flower fillings

UNLIKE ORIENTAL EMBROIDERIES, mine never have very neat rows of stitches; I prefer to stagger them slightly, as this makes the embroidery look less mechanical. Remember you are trying to copy nature not perfect it. Select the threads; several shades of each colour will be required. (I often sample blends beforehand on a spare area of ground fabric.) Using a water-soluble pen, make a tracing of the flower onto a fine fabric. Back it with a lightweight fusible fabric: the ground fabric must be strong enough to take the tension of both the hoop and the close stitching. Draw in any stitching guidelines that follow the growth pattern of each petal with a water-soluble pen. Then stretch the ground fabric on the smallest hoop available so that it is as tight as a drum.

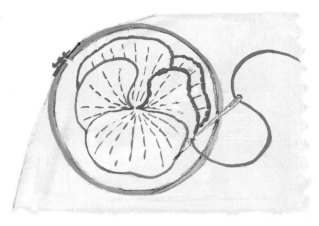

1 *With one or two mid-tone threads of stranded cotton (floss) stitch over the outline of each petal in either backstitch or split stitch to provide a firm edge to work over.*

2 5

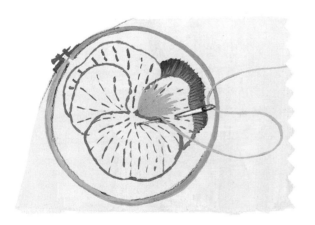

2 *To infill the petals, take one strand of thread to begin stitching, usually the palest; at the base of the petal make the first row of long and short stitches fanning them out towards the guidelines that have been drawn. Continue working the stitches out towards the petal edge, changing colours as you advance and blending them into each other with the long and short stitches. Take the last row of stitches over the outline stitch so closely as to cover it completely.*

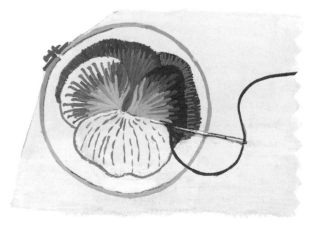

3 *Continue to work the other petals in the same way, taking care to preserve the overlap of the petals by means of the outlining stitches so that they appear natural. Finishing the centres of the flowers depends on the species: use French or bullion knots, couching or split stitch. Treat the leaves in the same manner as the petals, stitching along imaginary growth lines. Delineate the stem using a simple stem stitch; tram it first (see page 120) to make it look more robust.*

CREWEL WORK

THE MOST EXUBERANT FLOWERS seen in the history of embroidery must be those found in 17th-century crewel work. These exotic blooms were stitched in crewel wool yarns on very large pieces of linen, mostly for bed hangings and covers. Using modern tapestry and the finer crewel wool yarns on linen or heavy cotton grounds, a large crewel work can be created from the flowers in the book. There are several flowers already stitched in the distinctive patterns, both large and small scale, within the Floral Directory and a number of them have been put together to form a border for a linen curtain (see pages 48 and 49).

It is easy to copy and enlarge other flower outlines from the motif section and freely embellish them with special patterns illustrated in the Stitch Glossary, or you can use your imagination and invent your own designs. Finer and smaller crewel works can also be stitched in silks and cotton threads for a different look. The major embroidery techniques that give crewel work its specific character are rows of gradated colours in split or chain stitch.

26

crewel-work technique

TO WORK CREWEL-WORK designs, first copy the motifs and enlarge them as needed. Trace them on the ground fabric using a water-soluble pen and mount the fabric on a large hoop or stretcher frame so that the whole motif is visible. You will need to work the designs in crewel wool yarns that have an extensive shade range for each colour. This blending of colours is a major element in crewel-work design and gives a naturalistic feel to the embroideries while acting as a framework for the stitched patterns.

1 *With the embroidery stretched in a hoop, outline the key elements of the design in split stitch in the chosen colours, making sure that the sense of growth and the quality of the individual flower is kept.*

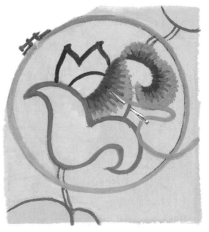

2 *Then start to fill in the outlined areas using patterns suggested on pages 135-137, or making up those of your own. Ensure the colours are evenly gradated, as this is fundamental to successful crewel work.*

leaf design

CREWEL-WORK LEAVES are usually worked in greens or browns to describe scrolling stems and turning leaves. This is often accompanied on the same leaf or flower with a freely embroidered design, either of a meandering plant or patterns using laid threads to cover the ground, held down with single threads couched with cross stitches.

This design is made up of long and short stitches for the gradated colours, with darning and cross-stitch infill, Jacobean laidwork and chain-stitched patterns.

27

flower design

THE PANSY OUTLINE has been traced from the motif section where there are many other flowers suitable to be enlarged and embroidered using this technique.

The first objective is to outline the flower and the second to fill in the spaces with any patterning that you want. Keep the colour palette quite limited, as lots of different patterns and textures can look garish, losing the sense of the flower's essential form.

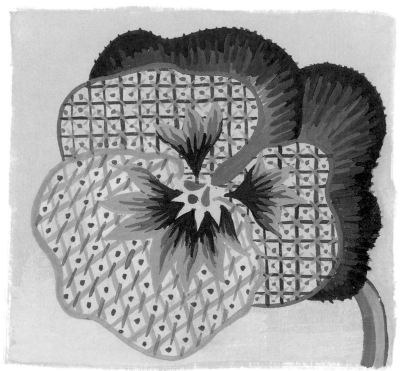

APPLIQUÉ

APPLIQUÉ FLOWERS ARE used extensively in this book; individual petals, flowers, stems and leaf shapes are cut from different coloured fabrics for embroidering, either by hand or machine. The fabrics used are either bought as a piece or more frequently ribbons are used (see pages 14 and 15). The wider ribbons can be cut into petals and even whole flowers, while the narrower ribbons are perfect for stems as they need no edge stitching and can be secured with running stitches or straight machine stitches. The use of iron-on fusible web as a bonding agent is always recommended, since it does two important things – keeps the cut motif permanently in place and stops the fabric edges from fraying. Although there are many stitching choices for securing appliqué, I use only two: hand- and machine-stitched buttonhole stitch.

preparation for appliqué

IT IS CONVENIENT if you ensure that all the fabrics and ribbons for any project have paper-backed fusible web applied to them prior to any drawing and cutting out so that the assembly can be carried out easily and completely as a preliminary stage, before embarking on the actual stitching of the embroidery.

1 *On a clean sheet of paper, lay all the fabrics and ribbons for the project face down. Cover them completely with a large sheet of fusible web, paper side up. Fuse the web to the fabrics using a warm iron.*

2 *Cut out the individual pieces of ribbon and fabric required for the appliqués. Trace the motif patterns required from the motif section and draw around the shapes on the back of the fusible-web backing paper.*

28

3 *Once you have drawn all the motifs you can start to cut out the individual shapes using a sharp pair of dressmaker's scissors. Be sure to cut out the shapes accurately to achieve a professional-looking finish.*

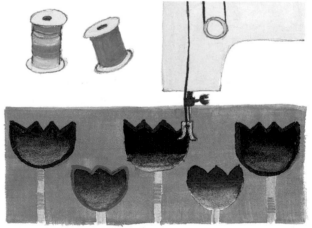

4 *Assemble the flowers on the fabric to be embroidered, stalks and leaves usually first, so that the flowers or petals hide the ends of the stalks. Remove the fusible web backing papers and press the flowers into position.*

hand appliqué

SIMPLE FLOWERS THAT rely on shape and colour are easily hand appliquéd using buttonhole stitch. Although the results are not refined, this particular look has its own charm. It is always best to work with the embroidery held in a position in a frame to ensure evenly worked stitches.

machine appliqué

THE STRONGEST AND MOST durable machine-stitched line for attaching a motif is a close zigzag or buttonhole stitch. It can be stitched to several widths and can be visually strong enough to be used as a line in its own right. The effect of this stitching gives a neat definition to the motif.

Stretch the fabric onto a hoop and, choosing a contrasting thread in a suitable gauge, work blanket stitch around each petal, leaf and stalk of the motif. Remember that when used like this, the embroidery is a drawing as well as an attaching technique. Finish off by working the details in the various stitches shown for the particular flower.

For straight lines and gentle curves, keep the presser foot in position. The solid quality of the line can be softened with a multi-coloured thread. A wide line will act as a factor in the design if contrasting colours are used to edge the motif, and very lively combinations can be made. However, you must ensure there are no visible gaps between the stitches.

THREE-DIMENSIONAL FLOWERS

THERE ARE A FEW FLOWERS in the Floral Directory that are free-standing; the manner in which they are constructed depends on the fabrics used and their eventual usage. The violet on pages 106 and 107 is the simplest to make as the velvet ribbons are bonded to a fine silk fabric, and, as the bonding adhesive prevents fraying, no further stitching is needed. The leaf could be treated in the same manner but would benefit from strengthening by sandwiching a heavy tailoring canvas between the back of the leaf fabric and a finer green backing fabric. Stitching the veins on the leaves will hold the sandwiched layers in place.

The little pansy on page 112 has had a heavy canvas sandwiched onto the back before being embroidered in blanket stitch, so it could be used as a brooch. The small bunch of auriculas in the Floral Directory is, in fact, a group of small blanket-stitched appliquéd velvet flowers that, like the pansy, have been cut out and wired together to make a single stem (see pages 94 and 95).

making and wiring a bunch of flowers

30

TO MAKE A bunch of auricula primrose flowers (or any other small bunch of flowers) you will first need to assemble the materials for six appliqué flower heads and one leaf (see page 95). You will also need enough millinery wire (or florist's medium-gauge wire) to create three lengths of 8cm (3in) and three lengths of 20cm (8in) to make six stems in all for the six flowers.

1 *Trace the designs from page 150 and bond the flowers to a fine backing silk using fusible web. Embroider the petal outlines (see page 94) and then cut them out.*

2 *Bend over the wire at right angles, about 1cm (¹⁄₂in) from the end. Wrap the wires with green thread to completely cover them. Then stitch them to the back of the appliqué flower as shown.*

3 *Make the next flower in the same way, but using the shorter length of wire. Then join the two stems together (see opposite).*

making leaves

YOU WILL NEED to make one appliqué leaf for the posy shown below. Three layers of fabric are bonded together with layers of fusible web; a top layer of satin, a middle layer of stiffer cloth (either tailor's canvas of felt) and a backing fabric or (use the top fabric again). You will need a length of wire to run down the back of the leaf and provide a small stalk. The leaf here is approximately 7cm (2½in) long and the wire 8cm (3in) long.

1 *Trace leaf design from page 150 onto the paper backing of a piece of fusible web. Press this to the back of the top fabric so that you have a rough guide where to place the wire in position on the central vein of the leaf. Remove the paper, leaving wire in position.*

2 *Place the heavier fabric on top of this and press wire firmly into position. Bond the backing fabric into position, press firmly with tip of iron around the central wire. Redraw the leaf aligning the wire with the tracing.*

3 *Finally, wrap the protruding stem with thread and buttonhole stitch the outside edge of the leaf in the same thread. Use small running stitches to indicate the central leaf vein.*

31

wiring a posy

WHEN YOU HAVE made up the individual components of the posy, you can put them together to create the little flower head. You will need to play with the positioning of the flowers to achieve a satisfactory balance. (If you want to display them in a pot, make up to four flower heads and three or four leaves.)

When you have achieved a satisfactory composition, with the small flower stalks creating an umbrella shape at the top of the plant, bind the stems together with more thread. Then attach the leaf stalk to the plant stem, binding that in position as well.

DISPLAYING FLOWERS

HAVING MASTERED THE techniques of embroidering flowers, you now need to consider how best to display them. The first thing to consider is the size and scale of the image, and how much of the ground fabric you may want to show. You should think, too, about the shape of the surround.

To make the most of a single flower from the Floral Directory you could surround it with a border of complementary fabric or ribbon. Using this method of design enables you to give a small embroidery extra emphasis and presence for a framed picture or, with the addition of several borders, a cushion. To do this, you need to think about the colours and the proportions of the bands that surround the work. Starting with the embroidery itself, look at the main colours used within it, and then find border fabrics that contain them. Make sure that the colours are a fair match in tone, by which I mean that these fabrics should not be so bright that they overshadow the embroidered motif, nor so dark or dominant that they make it look insignificant.

32

framing proportions

TO CHECK WHETHER you have chosen an appropriate size and form of frame for your embroidery motif, you can make rectangles from paper to create a movable frame, or you can use different-sized circular embroidery hoops. I like to see as little ground fabric as possible, as any frame should focus attention on the central motif and lots of background can weaken the impact. However, most embroideries will benefit from a subtle border to give the image definition and focus.

TO GAUGE *the appropriate size frame for a rectangular image, cut two L-shapes from a piece of thin cardboard. Move these into different positions to ascertain how much ground fabric to leave to best show off the image.*

HOOPS *are useful as gauges for a round frame. They come in different sizes, so try out several to see which shows the image off best.*

framing devices

SOMETIMES FOR an intricate or tiny embroidery a clear space needs to be left around it to let it "breathe", but it can still benefit from a subtle border to give the whole picture definition and focus. The simplest solution is to cut the embroidery background with pinking shears so that texture is added to an otherwise monochrome border; alternatively, you can stitch around the frame using herringbone stitch. On completing the embroidery back the area to be mounted with fusible web.

FOR A PINKED *edge, draw the frame in position using a set (try) square and a water-soluble pen; then cut along this line with pinking shears.*

FOR THIS FRAME, *the embroidery has been cut with ordinary scissors using a hoop as a guide, and then stitched with herringbone stitch in toning thread.*

fabric and ribbon borders

3 3

YOU CAN MAKE the same motif look totally different by the choice of ground and framing fabrics. In the two images shown here, the same little pansy has been embroidered (see page 43), but the choice of framing fabrics produces a very different effect. In both, embroidery ribbons and patterned fabrics have been used to extend the small image to make a much larger image, ideal for a cushion for example. Using ribbons successfully covers any raw edges. It is easier to overlap the ribbons at the corners rather than to mitre the edges.

IN THIS LIGHTER VERSION, *patterned fabrics with a lighter ground have been chosen creating a fresh, open look, with the secondary effect that the central motif tends to recede.*

IN THIS DARKER VERSION, *patterned fabrics with a darker ground have been used, with the result that the central image comes forward. Ribbon borders again cover the raw edges.*

LINEAR REPEATS

BY FAR THE MOST USEFUL DESIGN SYSTEM for embellishing fabrics is to repeat one or two motifs several times in a straight line. A good way to start is to make several tracings of the motif. If you are working in cross-stitch, a graph-paper outline is essential, and the motifs can be placed on adjacent squares. When working in stitches other than cross-stitch where the design and stitching is less regimented you may find that getting the flowers to touch one another so as to achieve a pleasing rhythm takes a little thought as the stems and leaves can easily become muddled; some "pruning" of the floral design might be helpful to create a more simplified outline.

It is usually simplest to design any repeat so that the motifs do not quite touch, but you have to use your judgement as to how closely to space them while still maintaining a sense of contact. When we design, we call the space in between the motifs "negative space" and it is as important a consideration in the overall image as the actual embroidered motif itself. If you allow too much space around each motif the design may look weak. If you allow too little the design may look cramped.

34

In the examples that follow, I show a few ways to create repeats, from single cross-stitch flowers in a straight line to a more complex spray motif where the central line of the motif needs to be established before the repeats can be worked, and ways to embellish lines to make more interesting borders.

simple linear repeats

THESE CROSS-STITCHED PINKS (see pages 68 and 69) on evenweave Aida braid are worked in a vertical line, each one positioned centrally above the preceding motif, with one intervening square. A more spaced-out design could be worked, leaving a few squares between each motif, but the character of the embroidery would then change. Much depends on the effect you wish to achieve. The more closely the repeating motifs are positioned, the stronger the effect.

To extend the design widthways, several lines of decorative herringbone stitches with bands of feathered chain stitches have been added on either side of the pinks. Stitches that complement the nature of the flower are best – here, the herringbone stitch echoes the points of the petals.

matching complex repeated motifs

TO EXTEND A COMPLEX FLOWER MOTIF into a linear design is relatively simple. Here the violets from page 108 have been used to create a pretty, fresh border.

Trace the design from page 108 and draw a line horizontally through the centre of the design. Draw a similar line in water-soluble pen on the fabric to be embroidered, extending it for the full length to be worked. Place the two lines together and pin. Then transfer the motif onto the ground (see page 18). Repeat the process to extend the line, moving the pattern paper along the length, adjacent to the previous drawing, making sure that the lines match. Repeat the process as many times as necessary.

adding a stitch border

TWO EMBROIDERED LINES of stitches, and a crochet braid fastened with herringbone stitches, add a fancy border to a pillow (see pages 46 and 47).

By keeping the design monochromatic the interesting patterns and textures of the embroidery are emphasized. The choice of a lacy braid and the delicate embroidery stitches – herringbone and detached chain – echo and emphasize the essential open character of the main embroidery design.

adding a ribbon border

IN THIS APPLIQUÉ alternating anemone flowers and buds have been positioned in a horizontal line. Toning ribbons have been added above and below the flowers.

To execute a similar design, cut out a few tracings of the two different flowers and position them on the ground fabric, drawing around them with a water-soluble pen. The join between the embroidery fabric and the borders has been hidden with narrow velvet ribbons.

35

BLOCK REPEATS

WHEN A LARGE PIECE OF FABRIC is wanted for a throw or curtain, the simplest solution is to arrange the embroideries rather like a patchwork, in neat rows and patterns. However, when a continuous pattern is required for an all-over effect, the flowers need to be placed harmoniously, void of big gaps and collisions.

Textile designers use a range of systems called repeats, and different repeating systems produce different effects. I find it helpful to make paper tracings or cut outs of the flowers that I want to use so that I can play with the spacings to be left between each motif. When deciding which repeating system to use it is worth considering the natures of the flowers: the character of an erect flower, such as the simple auricula primrose on pages 96 and 97, will retain its childlike appeal if kept to a simple regimented system that is known as the side-by-side repeat (formerly known as the full-drop repeat). The other two options are the half-drop repeat, where the rows of motifs are lined up vertically but staggered horizontally, and the brick repeat in which the half-drop pattern is laid on its side. You can, of course, vary the colours randomly or include the colours in the system of repeats you have chosen.

36

side-by-side repeat

THIS BASIC REPEAT is commonly used and is the simplest of all. The motifs are lined up with an even spacing between rows and between columns.

To arrange a side-by-side repeat you need to mark up the fabric to be embroidered with a grid, in which the spaces between the lines are large enough to hold the flower shape with a little space around each. Mark the squares with a water-soluble pen on the ground fabric, and find and mark the centre of each square. If you are using appliqué motifs it is best to back all the shapes with fusible web and then cut them out in advance, before pinning them in position. (The auriculas on pages 96 and 97 are laid out in a side-by-side repeat.) For hand or machine embroideries, mark the designs in the squares first.

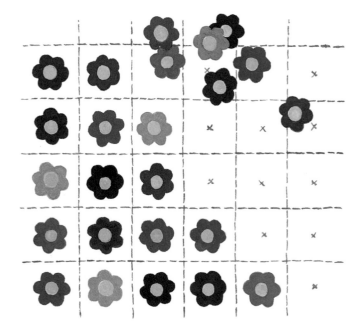

half-drop repeat

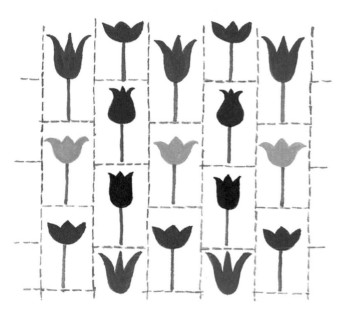

A LESS REGIMENTED and very common repeat is the half-drop repeat; the tulips on pages 104 and 105 are designed using this system.

Divide the fabric into vertical bands wide enough to accommodate the flower motifs and draw the lines with a water-soluble pen. Draw horizontal lines to make squares or rectangles, if necessary, down the first vertical column and in the next column draw another set of squares starting halfway down the first square. Fill in the rest of the piece of fabric with these guide lines.

Place the paper motifs in the squares and trace onto the cloth ready for embroidering, or use to establish where to put the applied flowers. Here the flowers have been arranged in bands of single colours.

37

brick repeat

TURNED ON ITS SIDE, the half-drop repeat becomes a brick repeat, with the motifs banded into straight horizontal lines. This is useful for designing borders on the edges of a tablecloth, where the motifs can get larger as they progress towards the hem, giving a good sense of weight to the border. (It has been used for the pinks on page 69.)

UPRIGHT MOTIFS *Neat linear motifs have been used for this simple brick repeat of tulips. The variation in the pattern is produced by using two colours in alternating rows, adding liveliness to the design without detracting from its neatly regimented order.*

ANGLED MOTIFS *You will achieve a greater sense of movement if the motifs are angled and the directions are reversed or if only the stalks move direction, as in the daisy design on pages 60 and 61. Extra space between the flowers gives the embroidery a more ethereal feel.*

COMBINING FLOWERS

IT IS ALWAYS EASIER TO DESIGN with just one flower at a time, as the flowers have the same characteristics embroidered in the same technique. However, many traditional embroideries, such as crewel work, have a mixture of flowers strung out along an undulating stem (see page 151 for a linear crewel-work border design). It is a pretty idea to combine plants to send a simple embroidered message using the language of flowers, which has been included in the individual descriptions in the Floral Directory. Or, just for the amusement of the embroiderer, you can play with the names of various stitches: what about combining a cornflower with a sprig of wheatear stitch? If you wish to embroider garden border pictures, the small flower groups on each page of the directory can be used to create a flower border (see opposite).

combining flowers in sprigs

SPRIGS OF FLOWERS are simple and quick to embroider and easy to arrange using the tracing paper method (see page 18). Simply choose some stems of flowers from the motif section and reduce them to a suitable size. It is a good idea to pick flowers and leaves with interestingly varied textures, and to ensure that the combination has an attractively fluid curve to the stems and the leaves. In the combinations shown here, the small violet has been combined with a delicate sprig of fern stitch, and the pinks with a little lavender spike. Make sure the design and the stitches marry well in style terms in either delicacy or strength.

VIOLET AND FERN *This delicate combination has an airy feel; in symbolic terms it conveys faithfulness (the violet) and modesty (the fern).*

PINK AND LAVENDER *These highly fragrant flowers would make an excellent choice for a scented sachet. The design and stitching of both is robust.*

38

combining flowers for a posy

FLOWERS CAN BE COMBINED to make attractive small posies. These daisies, for example, convey the message that here is a token of your unselfconscious beauty and innocence. The ox eye daisy indicates a "token", the part-coloured one "beauty", the white "innocence" and the red "unselfconsciousness".

Copy the designs from pages 60 and 61 using the tracing paper method on page 18, and arrange in a small bunch with the stalks crossing at one point. Place another tracing on a fresh sheet of paper, making sure that all the flower heads are nicely distributed. Mark this on the fabric ground using a water-soluble pen and embroider in the appropriate colours following the example of stitching from the Floral Directory.

combining flowers for a border

39

AT THE START of each description of a flower in the Floral Directory, there is an embroidery that shows the flower's growth habit in miniature, as if in the garden. While these make tiny pictures on their own, they can also be combined easily as they all are made using the same techniques, mostly long and short stitch and satin stitch.

In this little border the flowers are grouped in seasonal combinations, but as long as the colours go together and the comparative scales are sorted out anything goes. Follow the system described on page 19 for superimposing designs. You may need to use three separate tracings, however, rather than the two shown on page 19.

NAPKINS

THESE BRIGHT BUTTONHOLE and blanket stitch napkins are all in the Floral Directory along with the directions for stitching them: they consist of a pansy, poppy, anemone, auricula and a convolvulus. These embroideries are so simple that a child could make them; they simply require large needles and glossy pearl cotton threads. It is easy to find brightly coloured napkins in shops and stores, and any robust cotton or linen mixtures will do. It is easier to work the flowers on hoops, but the edges are simply stitched in the hand.

There are only five napkins in this set, but you can invent more by simply changing the colours – the convolvulus could be stitched in bright blue on a purple ground, the poppy in pink on a red ground or the pansy in orange on a violet ground: be inventive and clash those colours! Other flowers that could be added to the series are the hellebore on page 74, the pinks on page 70 or even a single flower from the hydrangeas on page 78.

Other ideas to create a set would be to use one flower stitched in all its different colours. The auricula would lend itself to this treatment, as its natural colour range is so varied (see the auricula appliqué on page 97 for inspiration or look through gardening books). Alternatively, stitch the different bright colours on pure white grounds. For a touch of elegance go the neutral route and stitch them all in cream on a dark natural linen ground.

40

right: *These brilliantly coloured linen squares are simply stitched in buttonhole and blanket stitch using contrasting coloured threads. They would be perfect for a bright set of napkins for a garden party.*

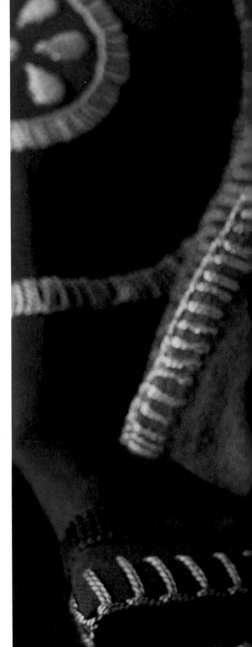

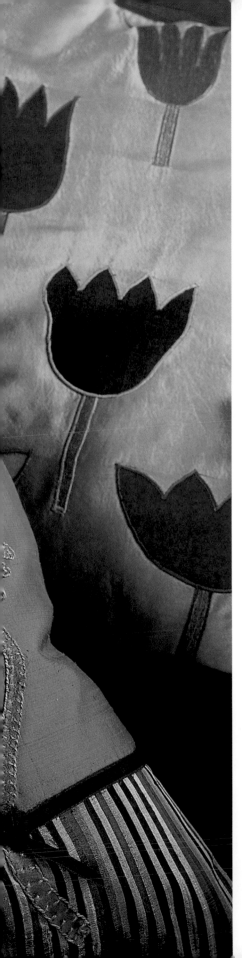

CUSHIONS

MANY OF THE FLOWER embroideries shown in the Floral Directory could successfully be made into cushions. I have made up a few of my favourites to demonstrate the different ways to employ them.

43

left: *These brightly coloured square cushions have all been made out of various designs from the Floral Directory. The tulips from pages 104 and 105 and the auriculas from page 97 are both machine-embroidered appliqués that lend themselves easily to cushions by the simple process of stitching bright silk backs onto the embroideries using one of the coloured silks employed for the flowers. The anemone is the hand-embroidered appliqué from page 58.*

above: *The small violet cushion (top left) has been made from the design on page 108, and bordered with velvet fabrics and ribbons to make a square shape, the colour of the velvets echoes the colours of the embroidery. The cross-stitch pansy (top right) is from page 112. It has been bordered with velvet and silk ribbons (see page 33 for designing ideas).*

APRONS

THESE GARDENER'S APRONS are all hand embroidered using the lavender, allium and fritillary flowers found as the main embroideries in the Floral Directory and worked to the size shown on the page. As all the flowers used have distinct outlines and visible detail, you can trace them straight off the directory pages using the illustrations as a stitching guide. If you want to make smaller or larger variations, refer to the techniques for transferring and enlarging or reducing on pages 18 and 19.

The motifs for the lavender and fritillary were drawn directly on the apron fabric and stretched onto an embroidery hoop for ease of stitching. The allium was drawn and then stitched on a separate linen rectangle (chosen to blend with the striped apron). This was made into a pocket by turning under the raw edges and top-stitching in position on three sides. You will need to use a piece of linen large enough to fit into an embroidery hoop, but you can then cut it to size for the pocket. Turn to pages 54 and 55, 72 and 73, and 82 and 83 for the information on stitching the flowers and for close-ups of the stitching detail.

right: *These linen aprons, hand-embroidered with softly coloured herbs and perennials, make an ideal present for an enthusiastic gardener or cook.*

44

PILLOWS

ALL THE PILLOWS pictured here are edged with embroidered borders that have been further embellished with extra rows of traditional hand embroidery for really special effects. When using purchased pillows you will need to undo a few centimetres (inches) of the open end by carefully unpicking the seams prior to applying the braids and embroideries. This way everything can be neatly finished off by sewing up the sides again when the work is complete.

The blue linen pillow has been embroidered using an undulating band of petal stitch (the pattern for this is given on page 151 in the motif section). Individual "lazy daisy" stitches are stitched as a further enhancement and a pretty length of crochet braid has been attached using herringbone stitch on one side and groups of detached chain stitches on the other. A design idea that is similar to this can be found on page 35.

The two other pillows are decorated with cross-stitched even-weave Aida braids; both can be found in the Floral Directory – the pinks are on page 70 and the roses on page 100. The pinks are attached by and embellished with rows of herringbone stitch variations and pretty double-feather stitch borders; turn to page 34 for other design details. The rose braided pillow has gingham-checked ribbon borders further embellished with a narrow ribbon couched in cross stitch.

left: *The pillows pictured here are embellished with rows of different types of embroidery, all of which can be found in this book. The best thing about embroidering your own designs is that you can choose just the right colours and details to match your own furnishings. These ideas can be adapted for many other flower embroideries in the book with the addition of different types of easily available ribbons and braids.*

47

CURTAINS

THE CREWEL-WORK flowers from the Floral Directory comprising the cornflower on page 62, the pinks on page 71 and the iris on page 81 have been joined together to make an undulating linear border for a curtain with the addition of a linking leaf design from page 145. The corner design has been simply achieved by the placement of the round pink flower at its exact point. The next leaf is at right angles to it, so the border will continue in this direction with the alternating flower and leaf combination. The patterns for this design are on pages 144 and 145 and 151 in the motif section.

To create a similar border, stitch it either on the curtain itself or attach the border to an existing curtain. I have used a neutral-coloured linen scrim, but it would be more traditional to use a richly coloured and patterned damask. Equally, you could edge a paisley or tartan throw with a similar crewel-work design. The design can be applied to the ground fabric so that a narrow border is left at the out-side edge and stitched in position with either ribbon or tape placed over the seam. Alternatively, you could embroider over the seams with herringbone stitch for a richer look. I have chosen to make a tape out of the selvages of the linen scrim and made simple, large running stitches with a multi-coloured woollen thread along the seams.

48

right: *This crewel-work border design can be extended by adding other flowers from the directory as only the outlines are needed for this type of embroidery; the patterns are put in at random according to the embroiderer's taste. The flower motifs used for the napkins on pages 40 and 41 would all work well for a design of this type.*

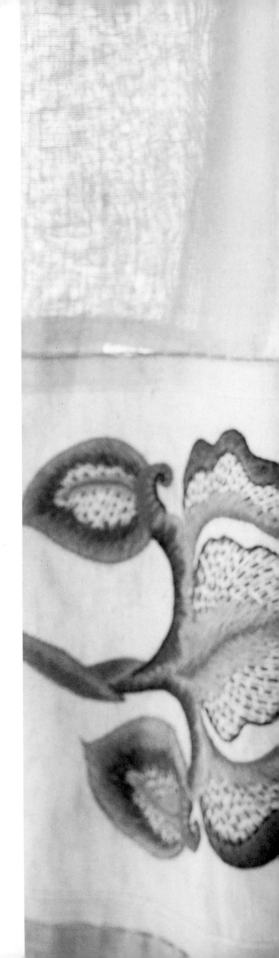

PANELS AND SCARVES

MANY OF THE DESIGNS are ideal for either scarves or panels. The long scarf shown here has been made by adding extra fabrics and ribbons to the poppy appliqué panel on page 92. As the poppies were made by cutting petals from wide silky ribbons, it was an obvious choice to use them as a border for the design.

Scarves need to be at least 1-1.5m (1-1^{1}/2yd) long to obtain a decent wrap and drape around the neck. I added several pieces of silk in similar colours to the ribbons used in the appliqué.

As the seams need to be smooth on the back, make them by placing the wrong sides together and machine stitching the seams, pressing them open at the front of the scarf and then hiding these with a ribbon over the centre of the join. If the back of the embroidery looks unsightly, simply back it with a very fine fabric in a toning colour and seam this at either end with the next fabric piece.

51

There are no hard and fast rules for this type of design, the proportions being decided by the width of the available ribbons and the colours of the silks that you can find. The design can have two matching ends if you make two separate pieces of embroidery: they need to be about 50cm (18in) wide. Keep adding more of them as you require, following this repeating pattern (the poppy appliqué pattern pieces are on page 151). When all the pieces are joined along the length, hem the edges by folding the fabric under twice, then press and machine top-stitch in a toning thread or invisible filament.

left: *The poppy appliqué from page 92 has been stitched to lengths of toning silks, the joins hidden by the addition of extra ribbons used in the appliqué with some vibrant velvet ribbons to add texture.*

the floral directory

The flowers have been chosen because they are those that I most often use for my designs as they are beautiful and adapt easily to embroidery. They employ a range of techniques and stitches, some incorporating several different techniques; many of them can also be successfully used for other design purposes. The flower embroideries should appeal to many different levels of ability. There are simple flowers for beginners, like the daisies and alliums, made up of the most basic stitches but enhanced by the choice of shaded and multi-coloured threads, and the hydrangea, where the silk ribbons do most of the work for you and are very quick. Even the elegant hand-stitched appliqué hellebore is made up of just simple running, split and seed stitches. The repeating designs of the tulip and auricula primula are an easy introduction to machine-embroidered appliqué while the hellebore heads, with their petals made from bonded silk ribbons, are a good introduction to hand-embroidered appliqué. Seasoned hand-embroiderers can perfect their techniques making the sinuous convolvulus or tulip embroideries, or try their hand at interpreting the glorious, variegated-colour combinations of the pansies.

ALLIUM

allium

These globe-shaped flowers are closely related to the onion and garlic family. Finding no reference to this particular plant in any of the language of flower dictionaries or my books of symbolic meanings I have bestowed on it the attributes of courage, strength and good luck.

above: flower group
A star of many straight stitches, radiating from the centre, was worked in a single strand of either green or soft red, then a scattering of tiny cross stitches in shaded threads of pinks and mauves form the flower heads. The buds are tiny ovals of trellis stitch. The long stems are single threads in stem and satin stitches.

opposite: *The large, round allium heads are made up of clusters of tiny star-shaped flowers, perfectly described by star filling stitches and French knots.*

54

AS THE FIRST FLOWER in this directory this is, fittingly, one of the easiest to stitch. The soft, hazy colours are achieved by using up to six strands of random and space-dyed stranded threads (embroidery floss) in various shades of pink, rust and mauve for the primary stars in each flower, overlaid with a second set of stitches in two strands of contrasting colour, in some flowers a vivid lime to grass-green blend. Both are worked in star filling stitch with a large French knot to finish in the centre of each "star".

The embroidery is worked in cotton threads on a linen ground so it is generally robust, but the big French knots might pull if the embroideries receive much hard wear. I have used them for the aprons on pages 44 and 45.

How to work the hand-embroidered alliums

1 Trace the motif from page 149, repeating as required. **2** Cut and bond into position three circles of fine gauze in appropriate colours. (The gauze is used to make a stronger impact, but if a really delicate motif is required, then leave it out.) **3** Work the stalks using narrow ribbons held in place with running stitches. **4** Fill the circles with star filling stitches, taking the outer stitches over the edges of the fabric circles to give a softer effect, and overlay with smaller star filling stitches in a contrasting colour. **5** Work a large French knot at the centre of each flower using six strands of cotton thread.

ANEMONE

anemone coronaria

In mythology the blood-red anemone is supposed to have sprung from the tears of Venus that mingled with the blood of Adonis as he lay dying; in the Language of Flowers they mean "forsaken" – such sad and curious associations for such colourful, cheerful flowers.

above: flower group
Using two strands of stranded cotton thread (embroidery floss), fill in the flower shapes in satin stitch, work a small star stitch in the centre and finish with a French knot. With a single strand of green work the foliage using long and short stitch and stem stitch.

opposite: *Three different versions of the anemone flower: the flowers in bud, a full-face flower and a side view.*

56

THERE ARE MANY different types of anemone but the jewel-like colours and sooty black centres of *anemone coronaria*, the popular florist's anemone, make for beautiful, vibrant embroideries. They can be bought as cut flowers in the very early spring. Watching anemones develop from large, round green buds, surrounded by their ruff of leaves, into pert, cup-shaped flowers never fails to inspire me. The little embroidery (above left) depicts the way in which the stems turn and twist, a key feature of these charming flowers. Machine-embroidered appliquéd flowers are shown opposite, with other variations on pages 58 and 59.

How to work the machine-embroidered appliqué anemones

1 Using a water-soluble pen, trace the flower design from the embroideries shown opposite and transfer this onto your chosen ground. **2** Cut separate paper patterns using the motifs on page 150 and, using these templates, cut the petals, stems and stalks from silk and bond them into position. **3** Embroider the petal outlines using a free-motion machine stitch with self-coloured threads. **4** Next, work on the centres, which are heavily spiralled and cross-hatched in black thread and then work the loops that are used to delineate the stamens. **5** The spiral twist of the stems can then be stitched in. **6** Finally, the frill of leaves can be freely embroidered in a scribbled pattern. As the silks used for the appliqué are fine and bonded to the background, the actual stitching is as much for strengthening as to give detail to the flower.

57

ANEMONE VARIATIONS

FOR EMBROIDERED VARIATIONS that rely principally on the wonderful colour range of the anemone rather than any intricacy of stitch, these simple hand-embroideries are ideal for embellishing tablecloths and napkins, or other household articles. The most robust is the full-faced flower on the linen napkin, opposite. The design of the three flowers lined up below relies on colour for its impact, but the curiously twisted stems add a rhythmical quality to this very basic hand-worked appliqué. The naive quality of this embroidery captures the simple charm of the anemone, and the brilliant colours and rich materials compensate for the loss of linear quality of the machine-embroidered samples overleaf.

The bonding of the velvet fabrics prior to the stitching of the raw edges means that they are suitable for use as a cushion or to decorate a bag. For developing it into a cushion design, see pages 42 and 43.

below: *These little anemones are cut from velvet ribbons and bonded to a contrasting silk ground before the flowers, petals and stems are hand-embroidered. They can be used as an edging, the motifs repeated as necessary.*

How to work the buttonhole-stitch anemone (right)

1 Enlarge the drawing on page 142 and transfer it to your fabric, making sure you record the varying width of the outline. **2** Choose a pearl cotton in a suitable thickness; here a single thread of No 5 is used. **3** Outline the petals in buttonhole stitch. **4** Use brilliant red (it contrasts well with the vibrant purple ground) to stem stitch the zigzag line surrounding the centre. **5** Use a black thread of the same gauge to fill in the centre using straight stitches in a pinwheel formation, working the stamens in straight stitches to radiate out with three rows of single chain stitches to look like the dabs of pollen stalk. (The stem and the edging are also stitched in the same gauge thread, but are doubled in the edging to give a more defined colour impression.)

How to work the anemone border (opposite)

1 Trace the anemone outlines from page 150 in the motif section. **2** Cut the petals and stems from velvet ribbons, backed with fusible web – ribbons afford a wider variety of colour and weight than velvet fabrics. **3** Bond the motifs to a coloured silk that enhances the brilliance of the flowers and embroider them using self-coloured No 5 pearl cotton thread, in blanket stitch, following the instructions on page 123.

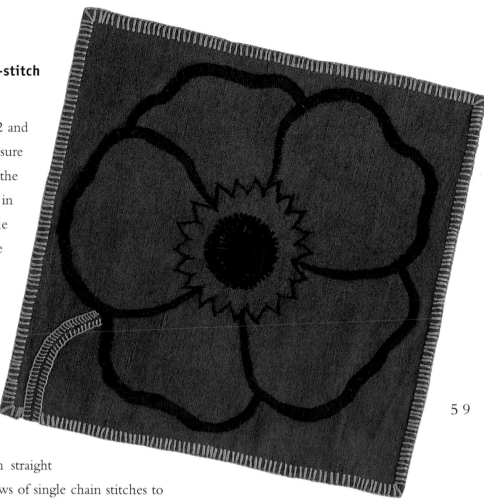

59

above: *This blown-up anemone flower has been used to make a table napkin. Different flowers can be used in the same way to create a set of them (see pages 142 and 143). The flower and the border to the napkin have been outlined in hand-embroidered buttonhole stitch.*

DAISY

bellis perennis

Surely one our most common and popular flowers, the "day's eye" name is a testament to how this little flower faces the sun, closing at night to open again the next morning. There are many different forms of daisy and many different colours. Depending on the colour and variety, different meanings are attributed to each flower; double daisies, for example, signify "participation" and Michaelmas daisies mean "afterthought"; of the colours, red-tipped ones indicate "beauty" while pure white flowers stand for "innocence".

60

above: flower group
This clump of flowers is worked in two strands of thread for the stem stitches and satin stitches of the leaves. Straight stitches are used for the petals in three strands of white thread.

opposite: *This elegant but simple design has been embroidered on a linen ground using No 5 pearl cotton in chain and detached chain stitches, French knots and Cretan stitches.*

THE LITTLE DAISIES shown here have been positioned in what is known as a "brick" repeat (see page 37). They are composed principally of "lazy daisy" stitches, which are, in fact, detached chain stitches, arranged in flower shapes either as full circles or semi-circles, or as upstanding tufts for the buds. You can trace the design from the embroidery opposite or make up your own repeating pattern.

Stitched around the edges of a tablecloth as a border, this embroidery design would look simultaneously fresh and nostalgic, as this particular stitch is every child's first embroidery stitch! The daisies would also make a simple and pretty edging for a pillowcase.

How to work the hand-embroidered daisies

1 Trace this design or create your own; work the white detached chain stitches first, leaving enough room to fit the red outlining detached chain stitches between them. **2** To fill the centres, work French knots in a greenish yellow (it enhances the rose pink of the outside petal colour). **3** Then work the stems and small leaves in detached chain stitch and the larger leaves (in the bottom row of flowers) in Cretan stitch.

62

CORNFLOWER

centaurea cyanus

The lovely shade of blue, and the naturally occurring pattern created by the overlapping scales on the calyx, have made this unassuming field flower a favourite with embroiderers since the 16th century. It can be found on bedspreads and cushion covers, purses and dresses – in fact, on all manner of embroidered surfaces.

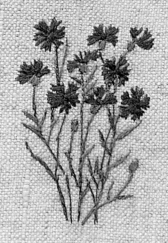

CREWEL WORK is an interesting embroidery technique to employ for this flower. It is designed here as a side view so that the handsome calyx can be seen and it is stitched in a traditional crewel-work stitch known as Jacobean laidwork. (The pinks design outline on page 71 can be adapted to become a full-faced version of this flower and was chosen for this reason.) The whole joy of crewel work is that many random patterns can be filled into the outlined shapes, so decoration is paramount. To this end you can play with different filling stitches to best depict the flowers.

The finished cornflower would make a hard-wearing cushion cover, or it can be placed with other flowers in a linear design as part of a traditional undulating crewel-work border.

How to work the crewel-work cornflower

1 Copy the motif shown on page 144 onto the ground using a water-soluble pen. **2** Outline the petals in split stitch using two strands of crewel wool yarn, which is quite fine. (This is important to achieve the point of the petals, which are part of the delicacy of this flower.) **3** Fill the petals with a variety of trellis and cross-stitch patterns, in turn filled with French knots in four gradated shades of blue. **4** Lay the leaves using large straight stitches fastened down with contrasting feathered chain stitches.

above: flower group
The elegant elongation of the stems and thin leaves are split stitched in single strands of thread. The flowers are groups of four straight stitches, one stitch radiating from the centre with a ray of three stitches describing the fan shape of the individual florets that make up each flower head, a star of deeper blue crossed over the centre.

opposite: *The cornflower was worked on a simple-weave linen ground using single strands of crewel wool yarns in shades of blue.*

63

CONVOLVULUS

convolvulus

This elegant flower with its distinctive, sinuous grace is actually a pernicious weed, but I suffer it in my garden because the flowers themselves are so beautiful. The field version is smaller and a pretty pink. Meanings given to this flower include "bonds and uncertainty" and "extinguished hopes".

above: flower group

The tall, meandering pink version of this flower is stitched in two shaded-cotton threads, pink through to white for the flowers and lime through to grassy green for the leaves. A single strand is used in the needle and the stems have been couched with satin stitches for both leaves and blooms.

THE CONVOLVULUS meandering over these pages is copied directly from a drawing that I made from a piece of bindweed I had pulled from a rose bush it was invading. It shows flowers, buds and a seed capsule with leaves spaced along the sinuous stem. The flowers have been stitched in blue to resemble those of its more glamorous cousin, known as morning glory (*Ipomaea*). The embroidery itself is simple: dependent on a strong linear drawing and meticulous stitching. It is a good piece on which to practice your embroidery skills! I used shaded threads in greens and blues to give variety to this essentially simple embroidery.

How to work the hand-embroidered convolvulus

1 Trace the drawing from these pages using a water-soluble pen and transfer it to the ground. **2** Using a finely twisted silk or cotton thread, stitch the outlines in appropriate colours. **3** Use running stitches to delineate the growth patterns of the petals and the veins on the leaves.

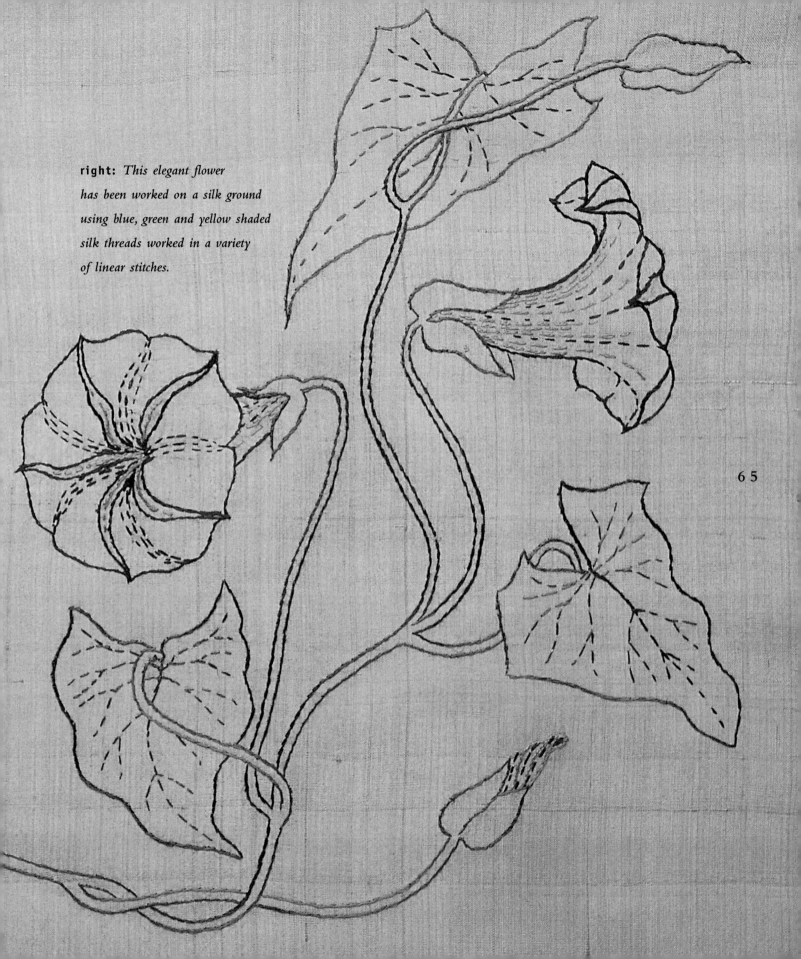

right: *This elegant flower*
has been worked on a silk ground
using blue, green and yellow shaded
silk threads worked in a variety
of linear stitches.

6 5

CONVOLVULUS VARIATIONS

THE RAMBLING NATURE of the convolvulus has been formalized in the design below into an elegant border. For the napkin opposite, the flower alone is depicted in buttonhole stitch to form part of a set of such designs (see pages 142 and 143).

How to work the machine-embroidered appliqué border (below)

This is made on two contrasting ground fabrics, a blue and a white linen. You can trace the motifs from the embroidery below and enlarge them. **1** Press a piece of fusible web onto the edge of the blue fabric and draw the undulating line that forms the join between the blue and white fabrics, then cut and press it into position on the white fabric. **2** Trace the convolvulus design and transfer it to the bonded fabrics. **3** Stitch the flowers and leaves

below: *This hardwearing appliqué would make an attractive edge to a pillow-case or tablecloth as it will withstand considerable wear.*

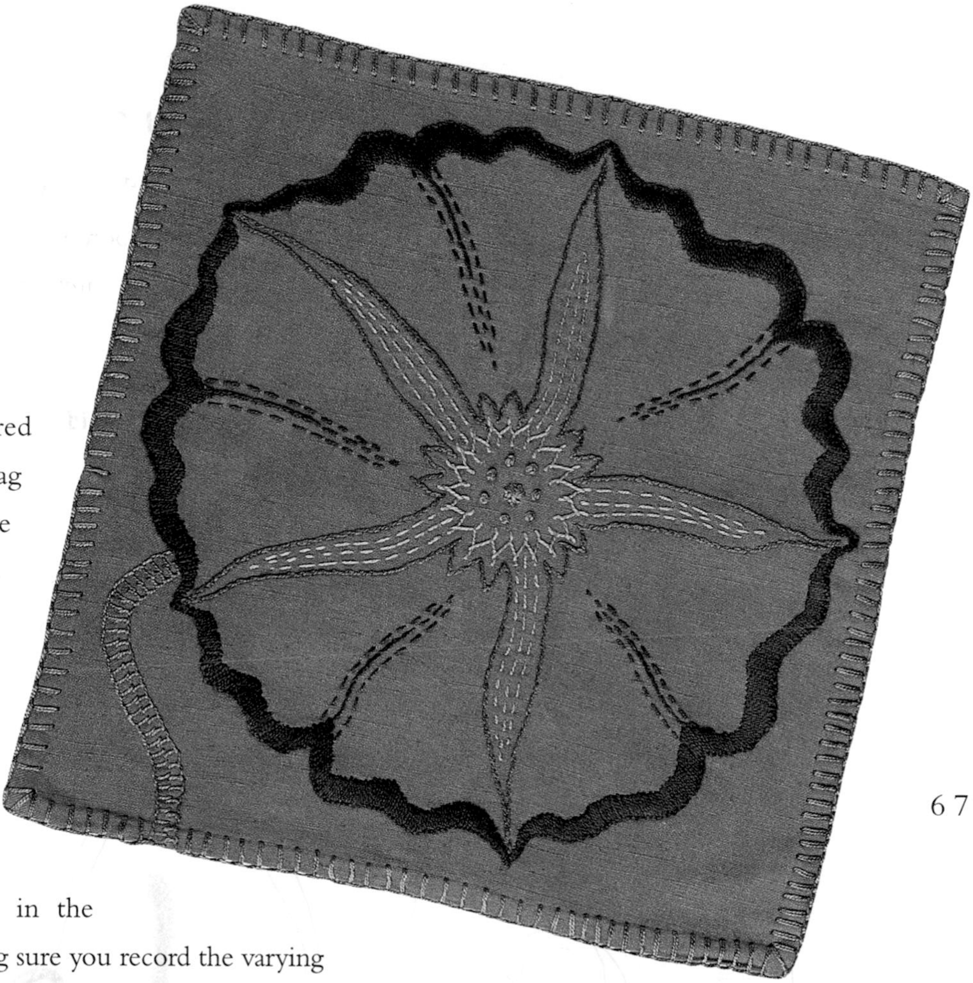

in position using self-coloured machine thread and a close zigzag stitch. **4** Stitch a wider zigzag line in green over the joined fabrics and then, in a narrower stitch, work the stems and veins of the leaves.

How to work the flower napkin (right)

1 Simply enlarge the drawing in the motif section on page 142, making sure you record the varying width of the line. **2** Choose a pearl cotton thread in a suitably heavy gauge. Here single threads of No 5 in two shades of bright pink and two shades of acid green were used. **3** Using bright pink, outline the petals in buttonhole stitching. **4** Work stem and running stitches in bright pink to create the divisions of the petals. **5** Work the paler pink lines between the fold indicators in stem stitches to create a star pattern. **6** Fill this star pattern with lime-green running stitches, and, for the flower centre, work narrow herringbone stitch in a circle. Then work large French knots to fill the centre. **7** Finally, work the convolvulus stem using two rows of buttonhole stitches. **8** Edge the entire napkin with buttonhole stitches.

67

above: *This simple but strikingly graphic design forms part of a collection of napkins using similar designs and stitches. The others are shown on pages 40 and 41.*

PINKS

dianthus

Pinks or carnations have traditionally been seen as the emblems of love and affection. However, in the language of flowers, the pink has many meanings, depending upon its colour. Red means "ardent" and "pure love", white means "talent" or "ingeniousness", and variegated blooms denote "refusal", obviously stemming from a time when this symbolism could be employed to send precise messages.

above: flower group

The flowers are made from two strands of cotton thread stitched in an irregular circle in long and short stitch, while small yellow star stitches complete the centres. The rather thin stems and leaves are made from straight stitches using a single strand of a bluish-green thread.

opposite: *These little cross-stitch pinks form a brick repeat pattern using three variations of flower style.*

68

PINKS HAVE ALWAYS been favoured by embroiderers and it is easy to see why; the stiff, straight stems and circular or, when seen sideways, fan-shaped flowers with their striped and spotted petals lend themselves to both flat and geometric designs. Looking through old counted-thread pattern books I found many different versions. The cross-stitch design opposite depicts fan-shaped flowers arranged in a brick repeat, using three basic designs, with the largest at the base. It is stitched on fine evenweave canvas, the cross stitches worked over every other thread. It could be adapted to many different uses if stitched through waste canvas onto other fabrics such as the hem of a child's cardigan or more simply on evenweave linen and made into the edging for a curtain, or a deep border for a tablecloth.

How to work the cross-stitch pinks

1 Refer to the brick repeat patterns on page 37 and the cross-stitch charts on page 146. The flowers at the base form the core of the repeat, with a five-stitch gap between each flower. (The cross stitches are worked over every other thread.) **2** Stitch the design on evenweave canvas using three threads of stranded cotton in shades of pink and green.

69

PINKS VARIATIONS

THERE ARE ONLY FOUR shades of pink used for the three designs shown here, the variety coming from the different stitches and techniques that can be employed to depict this versatile flower. The large crewel work opposite would make an ideal cushion cover, while the band of cross-stitch pinks on the left is perfect for a pillow edging and the little flat-faced pink below would make a pretty addition to the corner of a tablecloth.

How to work the crewel-work pink (opposite)

This is stitched in four gradated pink shades of crewel wool yarn using just a few simple stitches: split stitch for the outlines and for the stems and leaves, French knots for the background petals, and trellis couching for the infill stitches on the petals. **1** Trace and transfer the motif from page 145. **2** Outline the entire flower in the darkest red split stitch and then work in lighter shades to fill out the flower form. **3** Use French knots to fill in the background petals. **4** Outline the inner set of petals in mid-pink, using trellis couching or Jacobean laidwork for the infill stitches. (Note that the gradation of colours is carried through by the tiny straight stitches used to tie down the trellis.) **5** Use split stitches for the simple stem and narrow leaves. **6** Use a single strand of wool yarn for couching the curvy stamens.

left: *The large flower from the main design on the previous page has been repeated in a line and tied with a bow, on evenweave Aida braid, ready to be applied to the pillowcase on page 46.*

right: *This tiny sprig has been simply embroidered using radiating straight stitches for the flower and stem stitches for the leaves, in just two shades of pink and green.*

opposite: *This eye-catching crewel-work pink is given a graphic treatment in a limited range of colours and stitches.*

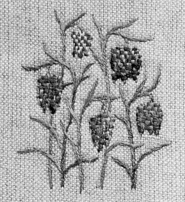

SNAKE'S-HEAD FRITILLARY
fritillaria meleagris

In the language of flowers, the snake's-head fritillary symbolizes persecution. This somewhat sinister-sounding meaning was probably conjured up by the unusual colours and markings, as they look vaguely reptilian both in the shape of the drooping head and in the purple, pink, green and creamy chequered markings that look a little like scales.

above: flower group

This tiny embroidery shows another crewel-work technique: weaving or darning. A single strand of green silk is straight stitched in tiny horizontal lines and woven across a single strand of reds and purples. Stem stitches are used for the foliage.

opposite: *Space-dyed silks with their delicately gradated colours are the perfect choice to capture the exquisite subtlety of these elegant little flowers.*

THESE DISTINCTIVE FLOWERS certainly create a challenge for the embroiderer and I have made many attempts to capture their soft colours and subtly checked patterns, which seem to slip and slide across the surface of each petal. The other challenge is to find a technique that will describe the variety of markings but also has the refinement to capture the plant's essential delicacy. Crewel work seems the perfect solution, as this technique allows for the creation of thin stalks and leaves. Leaving out the traditional outline on the flowers enables you to render their delicacy more successfully. Equally, using space-dyed silk threads, which are finer than traditional crewel wool yarns, creates a more ethereal result.

How to work the crewel-work fritillaries

1 Using a water-soluble pen, trace the embroidered image on the opposite page onto the ground fabric. **2** Using two strands of stranded silk or cotton (embroidery floss), or one of the finest crewel wool yarns, work the heads of the flowers using Jacobean trellis filling and its variations: the flower on the left of the picture was worked using Jacobean laidwork and those on the right with the laid threads tied down with St George's cross stitch. **3** Work the stalks and leaves in split and stem stitches.

72

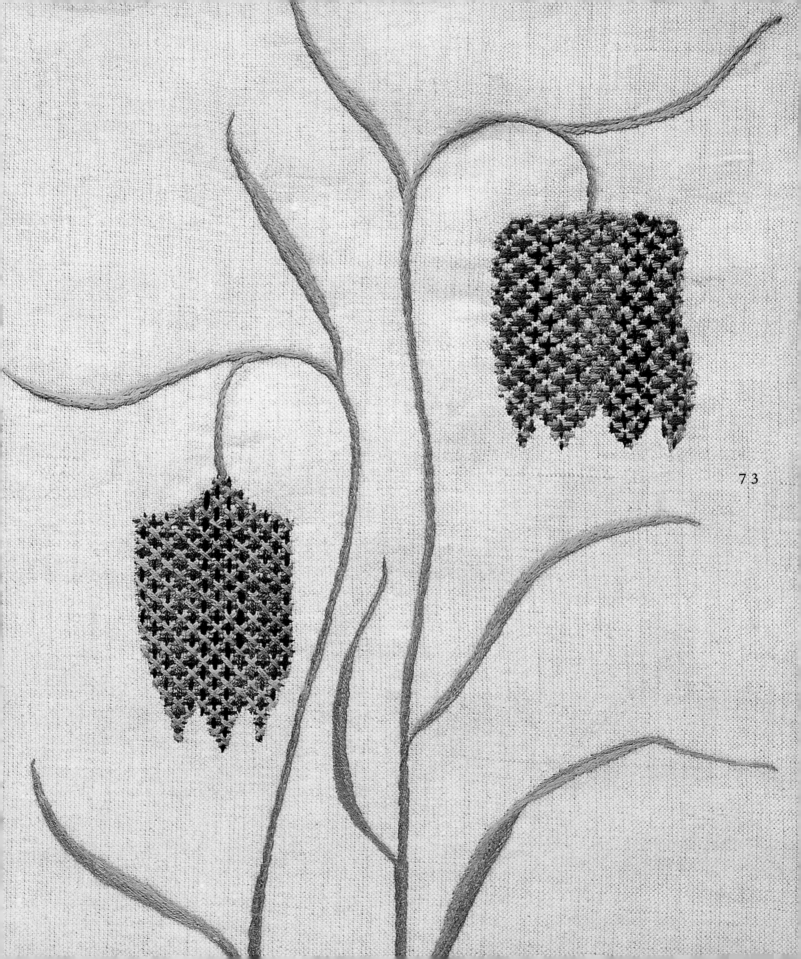

73

74

HELLEBORE OR LENTEN ROSE

helleborus orientalis

The hellebore can mean madness and delirium or scandal and calumny, depending upon the language-of-flowers dictionary to which you refer. Maybe the explanation for these negative connotations lies in the fact that hellebores are poisonous plants. However, despite these bad omens, the flowers are wonderful to embroider.

HELLEBORES, WITH THEIR handsome evergreen foliage, drooping flower heads and their subtle flower colours never fail to delight me. The colours can be difficult to capture, but the most successful results are achieved with multi-coloured, hand-dyed silk ribbons, cut into individual petal shapes and bonded to form each flower (see page 152). The fine fabric overlap suggests the delicacy of the flower.

How to work the hand-embroidered appliqué hellebore

1 Copy the motif on page 152, tracing the veins of the leaves and the dots on the flowers from the picture opposite. **2** Select a strong green ribbon for the leaves and stalks, and one with a reddish colour in its gradation for the stalks and bud. Back with fusible web. **3** Cut the same ribbon into three strips, coaxing the red edge into a gentle curve for the purple bud. **4** Assemble the flower and bud from any suitable ribbons (see page 76 for alternative colours) and press in position. **5** Using a deep green single strand of thread, split stitch the veins in the leaves following the vein tracing. **6** Using a lighter green strand of thread, make running stitches on the stalks and, using a deep red, dot the tiny running or backstitches on the petals. **7** Make the flower centres by backstitching circles of lime thread, and use single seed stitches in bright yellow for the stamens.

above: flower group
This tiny embroidery is made from stem and straight stitches. Like the embroidered appliqué opposite, it depends for its effect on multi-shaded materials, in this case space-dyed single strands of stranded silk thread (embroidery floss).

opposite: *Hand-dyed silk ribbons form the basis of this exquisitely simple hand-embroidered appliqué, the subtle colour gradations capturing the delicacy of the flowers perfectly.*

HELLEBORE VARIATIONS

THIS LARGE FREE-MOTION machine-stitched appliqué of full-faced flower heads has been assembled from hand-dyed silk ribbons organized in a side-by-side repeat on a fine gauze fabric. If the embroidery is likely to get some wear and tear – such as a scarf or shawl – lightly straight stitch the petal edges. For a blind or hanging, for example, this should not be necessary.

How to work the machine-appliqué hellebores

1 Use the motifs on page 152 to prepare your appliqué pieces. Then, using the picture opposite as a guide, assemble the flowers in a side-by-side repeat and press in position on the ground fabric. **2** Bond circles of green fabric to cover the gaps at the centre of each flower. **3** Positioning each flower on a small hoop (see page 23), machine stitch embroidery threads to depict the centres. (I used a selection of single threads of plain yellow and lime green with some variegated green through to bronze and yellow for a subtle but simple effect.) Using zigzag stitch, create the centre circle and the five large stamens in the same thread. **4** Changing to straight stitch, work the spiral in a different colour (inside the zigzagged circle). **5** Stitch the other stamens, making a few extra stitches at the end of each line for the pollen head.

77

left: *This simple side-by-side repeat of full-faced flowers gives the embroiderer full rein to show off inventiveness in the choice of subtle, harmonizing colours.*

LACECAP HYDRANGEA

hydrangea macrophylla

Beauty, without scent or fruit, heartlessness and frigidity are the traditional attributes of the hydrangea and, just for good measure, it is also designated as a "bad luck gift for a woman". So, should you choose to sample this voluptuous ribbon embroidery, perhaps you should keep the piece for yourself!

78

above: flower group

Straight and stem stitches are used for the branches of the flowering bush. Note the colour changes as the flowers appear on green stems above the brown woody branches; satin stitches are used for the leaves. Tiny cross stitches with French knots make up the flowers. The space-dyed threads can also be worked in deep or pale pinks, as hydrangea flowers can be either pink or blue depending on the soil conditions.

CHOOSING THE COLOUR blends of this embroidery was a real opportunity, as I have often looked at the glorious, speciality, hand-dyed, narrow silk embroidery ribbons (see page 13) and wondered how I could use them. To make this embroidery, use several separate ribbons in two different sizes in various shades from turquoise through to purple blues, with striated greens, pinks and violets for the flowers. The faded colours and softly wrinkling ribbon resemble dried flowers rather than fresh ones. Rayon ribbons would look fresher but the ground fabric would need a more open weave to allow the ribbons to pull through easily.

The resulting embroidery is very fragile. A box frame is best for mounting as considerable bulk is created at the back of the ground fabric.

How to work the ribbon hydrangea

1 Trace the pattern from the motif on page 148 – the number of petals in each floret varies between four and five. **2** Work the florets in ribbon stitch (see page 138), following the embroidery opposite for the colour variations. **3** Using space-dyed threads for the little central buds, flower stalks and stems, work the central buds as small clusters of French knots using three strands. **4** Work the flower stems in stem stitch using one strand. **5** Work the lower, thicker stems in trammed stem stitch using two strands.

above: *This delicate ribbon embroidery is finished off with a bow, turning it into a little posy.*

IRIS

iris variegata

In Greek legend, Iris was the messenger of the gods and her path through the heavens was visible by the rainbow she left in her wake. This, then, is the reason that the iris spells "a message" in flower symbolism. From the earliest times, the iris flower has been associated with a myriad of colours: the word "iridescent" comes from the same source.

80

above: flower group
The small group of flowers shows the handsome sword-shaped leaves that are part of the beauty of the iris grown in the garden. Pale blue combined with dark blue is typical of the common iris, but yellow is also usual as a colour in the wild varieties. Satin stitches worked with two strands of thread are used for this embroidery.

opposite: *The stitching of patterns has been kept to a minimum to show off the colour gradations.*

THE IRIS has a long tradition in flower embroidery and can be seen in many different versions throughout the history of crewel work, from the 17th century to the present day. The softly gradated colours of the iris petals lend themselves beautifully to the crewel-work technique. You can blend the shades of each colour in long and short stitch or encroaching satin stitch for a smooth transition.

How to work the crewel-work iris

1 Using a water-soluble pen, copy the tracing on page 144 and draw the guidelines for the stitch directions. **2** Work the flower outline in split stitch to keep the undulating quality of the petals. **3** Using the illustration opposite as a guide, blend the range of mauves on the lower petals and work a line of blanket stitch on the two curving lines where the flower emerges from the calyx, using one strand of crewel wool yarn. **4** Work the greens for the calyx and all the other petal blends within the outlines, put in the other rows of blanket stitches on the yellow curvy petals. **5** Work the central yellow blend of the main petal and the two other upper outer petals and then amalgamate the two sets of colours by working even running stitches in alternate shades towards the outside edges of the petals.

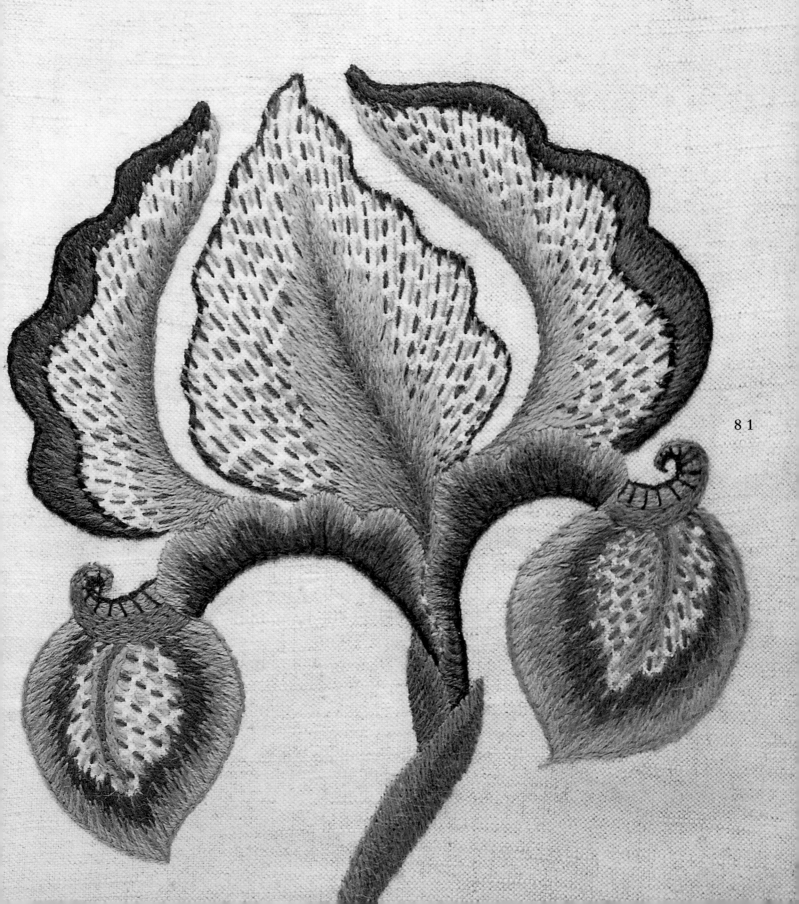

LAVENDER

lavandula

Constancy and loyalty, sweetness and undying love are the traditional attributes of this little herb, whose purifying and soothing properties have long formed part of herbal medicine. The sweet scent of dried lavender flowers is often used to perfume household linen and lavender itself is seen to be a "good luck" gift to women.

82

above: flower group
Straight stitches in single strands of brown and green, threaded together in the needle, form the woody base of the plant. Small satin stitches in soft green make up the foliage and the long stems while the flowers are embroidered in chain or buttonhole stitches in shades of pink or purple.

IN KEEPING WITH its reputation, lavender is the natural choice to embroider onto natural hardwearing linen as a useful gift for the home. The embroidery shown opposite is very simple, depicting two different forms of lavender: English and French lavender. It is worked in just a few stitches: stem stitch for the stalks, satin stitch for the leaves and detached buttonhole or chain stitch for the flowers. It has been transformed by the use of several different space-dyed threads in shades of green, purple and red. Only two strands of thread are used throughout this embroidery.

How to work the hand-embroidered lavenders

1 Using a water-soluble pen, trace the design from the page opposite. **2** Work single buttonhole or chain stitches to describe the individual lavender flowers clustered at the top of the elegant stems: make single stitches in soft mauves and pinks to form the base of each flower, then make two or three loops attached to them in stronger colours. **3** Tram the stems prior to stitching them in satin stitch. **4** Use satin stitch also to depict the leaves.

opposite: *These little sprigs of lavender can be embroidered individually onto a lavender bag or grouped together, as on the aprons on pages 44 and 45.*

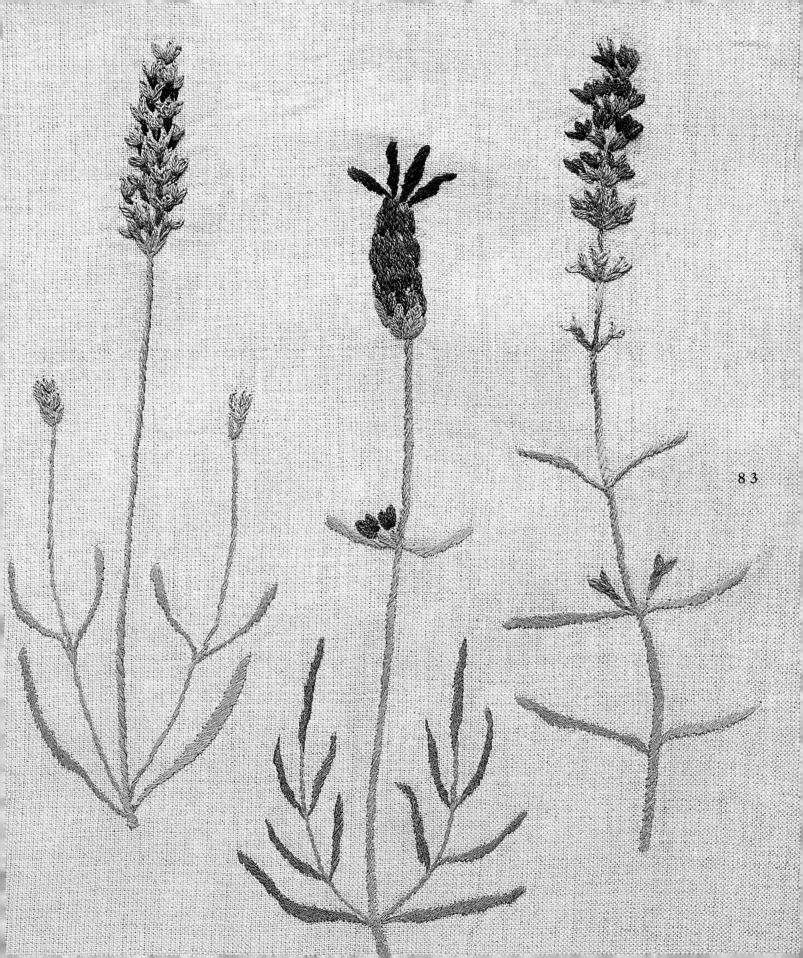

8 3

left:
Ombré-dyed ribbons have captured the delicacy of the sweet pea flowers, while the free-motion machine stitching admirably depicts their growth pattern.

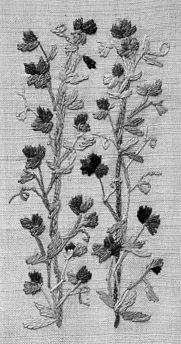

SWEET PEA

lathyrus odorata

In the language of flowers the sweet pea means "departure and adieu", which makes it a good flower to embroider for a leaving present. However, the lovely scent always reminds me of my childhood, when seasonal bunches of sweet peas were sold alongside the fruit and vegetables in our village shop.

THE SUBTLE COLOURS that make this free-motion machine-embroidered appliqué so delicious are achieved by using two ombré-dyed ribbons for the petals and a solid pale green ribbon for the leaves and lower thickened stems. The outlines and tendrils of the sweet peas have been stitched in a fine-gauge, shiny rayon thread.

How to work the free-motion machine-stitched sweet peas

1 Prepare the appliqué pieces using the motif on pages 154 and 155. **2** Position the ribbons over each petal so the colour shades from the palest at the base to the deepest at the outer edge. **3** Bond the ribbon pieces in position and stretch a small area in a hoop ready to stitch (following the technique on page 23). **4** Using a blend of pink threads, stitch one group of flowers first, and then reposition the hoop to embroider the next. **5** Change to green threads to work the stems and leaves. **6** Finally, machine stitch the heaviest central line of the stems using a straight stitch with the presser foot in position (heavy thread is too thick for the ease of movement required for free-motion machine stitching).

above: flower group

Stranded cottons (embroidery floss) in four shaded colours are used here; long split stitches of two strands for the canes and stalks, and single strands for the satin-stitched oval shapes that form the basis of the flowers and leaves. The tendrils are couched. It is the choice of colours and the overall shape of the plant, rather than the look of the individual flowers, that are important.

85

LILY

lilium

The pure white lily is a symbol of purity and chastity while the yellow lily is one of falsehood and gaiety; care really needs to be taken when sending messages using the language of flowers!

above: flower group

The variegated buds have been created using two different coloured single strands in the needle together; a lime green and a rose-red. Paler pink and green threads have been used together for the slightly open flowers and a single colour for the fully open flowers. Stamens are stitched in vivid green with rose-red used for the pollen heads.

8 6

THE SPOTTED LILY depicted opposite was chosen to show how a refined line drawing can be embroidered in subtle colours but still be as rich and detailed as a fully embroidered flower. The secret is to have a good drawing with a strong outline as a base, and trace it directly onto the background using a water-soluble pen (see page 18). Any flower chosen for this style of embroidery must have a clear silhouette and some additional feature that offers extra information about the flower: the spotting on these lilies helps to add decorative effect while also indicating the overall shape of the petals. In this embroidery the deep pink dots are stitched using a combination of dot and double dot stitches so that they follow the curve of the fullness of the large petals. The central split- and running-stitched lines of the smaller petals are used for the same effect.

How to work the hand-embroidered lily

1 To achieve lines fine and smooth enough to describe the undulations of the petal, work the split stitches using a single strand of stranded silk (floss) and ensure that the stitches are shorter than 5mm (^{3}/$_{16}$in). Around the tight curves, such as the petal tips, this reduces to a length of 2mm (^{1}/$_8$ in). **2** To smooth out the slight jaggedness as the stitches describe a corner, it is best to whip the stitches (see page 137). **3** To describe the leaves, use two threads, working them in the same split stitch and whipped combination. **4** Work the stamens and stigma in stem and satin stitches respectively.

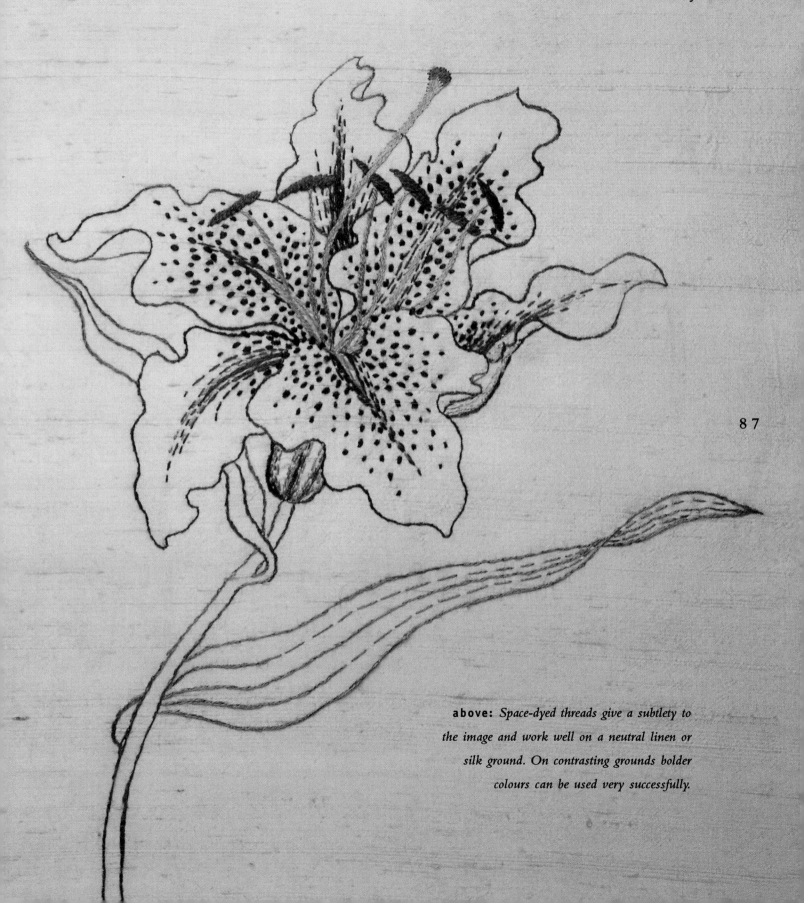

87

above: *Space-dyed threads give a subtlety to the image and work well on a neutral linen or silk ground. On contrasting grounds bolder colours can be used very successfully.*

NARCISSUS

narcissus

The story of Narcissus, of how a handsome boy fell in love with his reflection in a pool, is one of the best known Greek myths. Legend has it that when he died of grief, a flower with a white circle of petals around a yellow centre grew at the water's edge. In the European language of flowers, the narcissus is a symbol for egotism and conceit, but in Japanese and Chinese symbolism where Greek culture has played no part, the flower means good fortune and joyfulness.

above right: flower group
Satin stitches form the petals around a deeper coloured star-stitched centre, while stem stitches are employed for the thin stems and stalks.

opposite: *These elegant little flowers could be repeated to make an attractive border for a blind or hanging.*

THIS ELEGANT EMBROIDERY is an appliqué in which a two-tone silk has been used for the leaves and stalks, and a pure white silk satin for the petals, with yellow silk for the centres, all machine stitched with variegated threads. In this embroidery the stalks and leaves were cut from wide ribbon and the flowers from fabric scraps.

89

How to work the machine-stitched appliqué narcissus

1 Trace the flowers from page 153 and the leaves from the opposite page, and cut them out of the fabrics, previously bonded on the back with paper-backed fusible web. **2** Position the appliqué on the ground fabric and press in position. **3** Draw the stitching details onto the fabrics with a water-soluble pen, particularly the wavy line around the flower centres. **4** Stretch the fabric onto a small hoop and, using a straight stitch, outline the petals with an orange-yellow thread, stitching the line twice. **5** With the presser foot down, straight machine stitch the details onto the leaves and stalks using space-dyed green thread: here the colours range from green through yellow to mauve: quite a soft set of colours. **6** Stitch a star for the flower centre detail, then outline the centres in a close zigzag stitch.

POPPY

papaver

Imagination and dreaminess are the symbolism of the poppy, which comes in many forms, from natural field poppies to elegant opium poppies and the large-flowered Oriental poppies with their wonderfully blowsy petals.

above: flower group
The growing poppy plant can be stately, with lovely blue-green foliage, or meandering, as with the Oriental poppies above. The satin-stitch petals have black cross stitches and French knots at their centres, with small straight stitches to denote the dark blotches of the petals at the base of the silhouetted flowers.

90

opposite: *The strong graphic lines of this delightful appliqué create an arresting image.*

IN THIS EMBROIDERY of an Oriental poppy, the characteristically crinkly appearance of the petals has been rendered with a silk chiffon that assumes this quality when dampened, left to dry, and allowed a naturally frayed edge. The leaves and stalk are cut from wide, shaded green ribbon. Hand-embroidered running stitches in silk threads secure the appliqué to the ground fabric. This is not as difficult an embroidery as it might appear, but it does involve the manipulation of the individual parts, as the petals have two layers – a silk under-petal that is cut to the petal shape and a second, slightly larger piece of transparent silk that is gathered onto this at the centre (see page 151 for patterns and instructions). However, having made several of these for many different embroideries, they never fail to delight anyone who sees them.

How to work the hand-embroidered appliqué

1 Trace the flower and bud petals ensemble, baste the petals and one bud to the ground fabric. **2** Bond the leaf, stalk and bud fabric to the fusible web, then trace, cut and press in position. **3** Using a single strand of silk, secure the petals in place with running stitches, following the rhythm of the crinkled fabric. **4** Work the central star in heavy dark-red silk thread and then work the anthers in the same thread. **5** Secure the stem, leaves and bud using running stitches following the natural line of growth. A small sliver of silk has been trapped inside two halves of the bud.

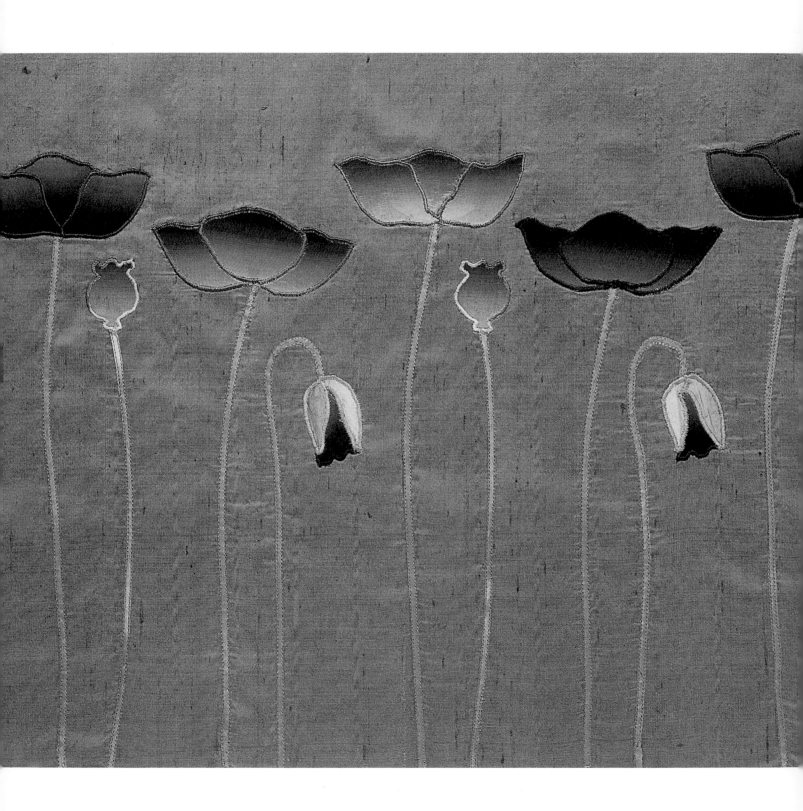

POPPY VARIATIONS

THE RICH COLOURS and stately growth of opium poppies have been captured as a machine-stitched appliqué (opposite) and, in a very different vein, a single hand-embroidered colourful flower makes a dramatic statement on a napkin (below).

How to work the opium poppy appliqué (opposite)

1 Using a water-soluble pen, trace the pattern for the flowers on page 153 (seen in repeat here) onto a silk ground. **2** Cut the individual petal shapes from wide, gradated, dyed-silk ribbons and use narrow silk embroidery ribbon for the stalks. **3** Baste in position using the image opposite as a guide. **4** Use close machine zigzag or buttonhole stitch in like colours to delineate the flower heads. **5** Use straight stitches to secure the stems in place.

How to work the
buttonhole-stitch napkin (right)

1 Enlarge the motif on page 153 and trace it onto the ground using a water-soluble pen. **2** Follow the stitching instructions for the anemone napkin on page 59, using a scarlet heavy pearl cotton thread for the outline, satin couching for the stem and French knots for the centre.

opposite: Embroidered on a rich silk dupion ground, these opium poppies in gradated silk ribbons with their delicate slender stems, make an exquisitely elegant panel or throw (see also page 51).

93

right: *The poppy flower, seen full face, makes a striking graphic image for a set of table napkins.*

AURICULA PRIMROSE

primula auricula

Auriculas are the quintessential designer's flower. When first encountered, they do not look real. In fact, they look exactly as though they have been manufactured from fabrics! The colours are brilliant and varied, the yellow centres and stamens surrounded by a flat circle of either white or yellow from which spring the small, even, rounded petals. Unsurprisingly, in the 19th-century language-of-flower books, they symbolize "painting".

above: flower group
This group of flowers is seen growing from the ground but quite often auriculas are grown in pots. The individual tiny flowers are made of satin-stitched petals with a voided white ground at the centre and a star stitch in yellow for the stamens. The large leaves are also satin stitched.

opposite: *This three-dimensional auricula would look charming placed in a small plant pot.*

94

THE RANGE OF COLOURS that can be found in these flowers includes the whole gamut, some having attractively coloured edges. For other colour variations turn to pages 96 and 97. Here the flowers have been made totally three-dimensional. The embroidery can be mounted in a box frame or the technique can be used to create a brooch. The thread used for this embroidered edging is a pearl cotton.

How to work the three-dimensional appliqué flower embroidery

1 Trace the motif on page 150. Transfer the flower heads to fine velvet: (a ribbon would be ideal). 2 Use fusible web to bond them to a stronger fabric before cutting them out. 3 Then iron them onto a finer fabric such as organza or lawn, which is stretched on an embroidery hoop so that you can work the hand stitches. 4 Next, define the petals using small blanket stitches that also cover the edges of the petals. 5 Straight stitch the circles of white silk in position with a single strand of silk. 6 Render the yellow stamens in bullion stitches. 7 Finally, cut the finished flowers and wire (see page 30). 8 Make the leaf by tracing the motif on green silk, and buttonhole stitch the edging. Wire it as shown on page 31.

AURICULA VARIATIONS

HERE A SMALL colour range of auriculas has been cut from brilliant silk habutai and assembled into a simple side-by-side repeat (see page 36) and machine embroidered in self-colours using a close zigzag or buttonhole stitch in heavy-gauge embroidery silk. The napkin above is another version of those shown on pages 59, 67, 93 and 113. The tiny floret, right, is stitched in long and short stitches and stem stitches.

above: *This full-face auricula flower stands out against the ground fabric. It is worked in two stitches: buttonhole for the outline and satin stitch for the centre.*

opposite: *A side-by-side repeat is used to display these graphic floral images, which are simply machine stitched on a stunning dark silk ground.*

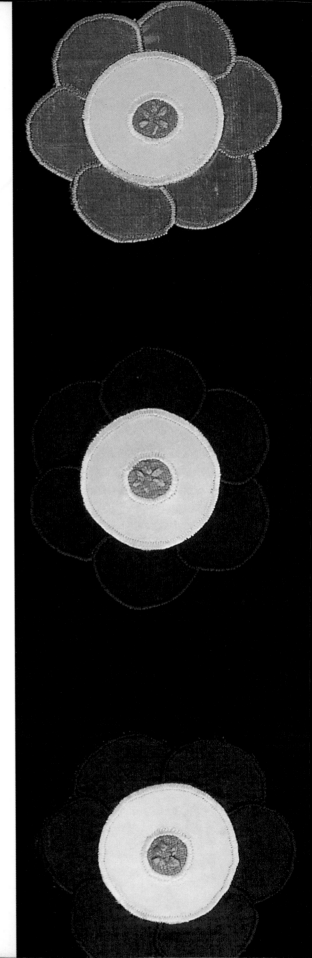

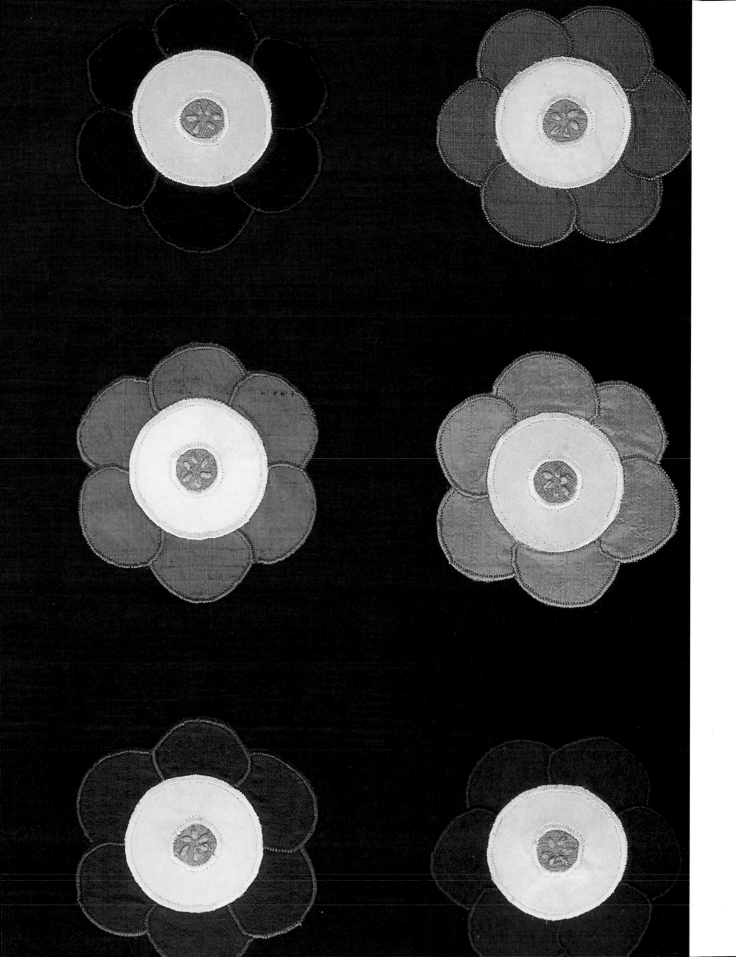

98

ROSE

r o s a

Roses, as we all know, symbolize our love and affection, but there is a whole host of different meanings given for the rose depending on whether it is in bud or in full bloom, single or double, and according to the variety, the colour and so on. One dictionary lists no fewer than 40 different types and attributions. However, in general red is for purity and loveliness, yellow for jealousy and white for worthiness.

ALTHOUGH ONE OF the most beautiful and popular flowers, appreciated throughout the world, the rose is not one of my favourite flowers to embroider. However, there are so many variations in embroidery that go back for centuries that it seemed worth suggesting some techniques that are both simple and effective. Cross-stitch designs really make the difficult-to-capture, enfolding quality of the full-blown rose easy to attain, as this subtle, shaded embroidery shows. I have used this particular design motif many times. There is only one spray motif here, used first upright and then repeated but turned at right angles, with a little leafy shoot to achieve a more elegant design. The softly coloured wool yarns help to make these blooms look faded and old-fashioned. They would look good worked on a velvet ground using the waste canvas technique on page 24.

How to work the cross-stitch rose

1 Trace the chart on page 147. **2** Using two strands of crewel wool yarn, work each cross stitch over five threads of 28-count evenweave linen, stitching the flowers in five shades of mauve and five shades of yellow. **3** Use four shades of green for the leaves and one shade of brown for the stem.

above: flower group
This standard rose is made from groups of bullion knots in two shades of pink thread, with detached buttonhole stitch for the leaves and satin stitches for the trunk and branches.

opposite: *Soft, shaded colours help to give this little cross-stitch rose the appearance of an old-fashioned variety, distinguished by its wonderfully faded soft colours and delicate petals.*

99

ROSE VARIATIONS

HERE ARE A few ways to capture the essential quality of rose petals: one is a cross-stitch design, another a ribbon design, and the third a free-motion machine-stitched wool embroidery.

How to work the cross-stitch band (far left)
1 Trace the chart on page 146. **2** Work the motif with three strands of stranded cotton (embroidery floss) on Aida braid: the rose and bud in three strands in three shades of pink. **3** Work the leaves and stalk in three strands of gold.

How to work the space-dyed ribbon border (left)
1 Work the flowers on a velvet ribbon using spider-web rose stitch (see page 139) and two colours of space-dyed ribbons, which give a feeling of depth to this simple technique. **2** Work the green leaves in ribbon stitch (see page 138).

How to work the free-motion machine embroidery (right)
This free-motion machine embroidery uses a thick but delicate chenille thread that must be wound by hand onto the bobbin (see page 22). As the loosely woven wool ground is difficult to draw on with any pen or chalk, draw the design on a piece of tissue paper and baste it to the back of the fabric instead of bonding on a fusible backing. (This is not a disadvantage as this technique requires the design to be stitched from the back.) **1** With the chenille thread on the bobbin and a colour coordinated, space-dyed thread threaded through the needle, straight stitch over the drawing of the flowers. **2** Change the colour and repeat for the leaves. **3** Pull away the tissue when the embroidery is completed.

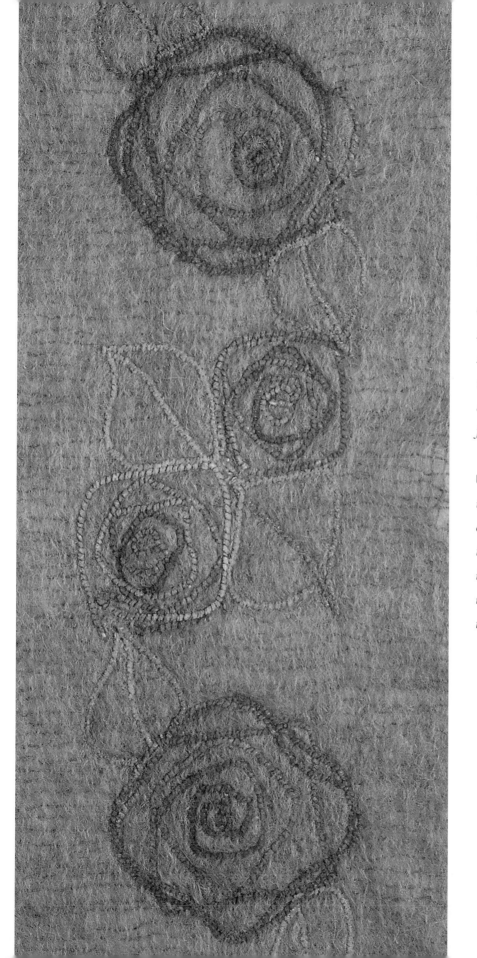

opposite (left): *This attractive little cross-stitch border would be ideal for bed linen.*

opposite (right): *Simply stitched using two ribbon stitch techniques, this elegant rose band would make an attractive necklace or a border for knitwear.*

left: *This free-motion machine-stitched wool embroidery has a '30s feel to the design. It is stitched in delicate chenille threads using a special machine technique (see page 22).*

1 0 1

TULIP

tulipa

Tulips have always attracted attention with their elegant heads of waxy petals, some slender, some frilled and some striped or even multi-coloured. In the language of flowers a variegated tulip means "beautiful eyes"; a red tulip indicates a declaration of love, while yellow, on the other hand, means "hopeless love".

above: flower group

This upright group of multi-coloured tulip flowers and leaves is worked in satin stitch and stem stitch with two strands of stranded cotton (embroidery floss).

102

THE TULIP HAS BEEN in cultivation for centuries and at present the variegated forms and striped forms are particularly popular. The plant has two different characteristics: when growing it is upright and neat in its habit, but once picked and placed in water the stems start to twist and undulate, and the petals flare out, producing sinuous and curving lines that make elegant embroideries.

In this embroidery, the softly coloured and sensuous flower is striped in a gradated range of single-strand mauve silk threads with the leaves worked in gradated greens. The background fabric within the flower shape has been left unworked (voided) to act as the ground colour for the flower. The long and short stitches follow the growth pattern, but the leaf requires careful manipulation of the space-dyed threads to give the quality of movement to the fold in the leaf.

How to work the hand-embroidered tulip

1 Trace the motif from page 149 and transfer it onto the ground fabric using a water-soluble pen. **2** Work the petals, following the striped pattern opposite, using long and short stitches. **3** Stitch the leaf outline and the fold divisions in split stitch. **4** Tram the leaf and infill with encroaching satin stitches. **5** Tram the stem and work in satin stitch.

this page:

*The darker coloured threads
used for the background
petals of this elegant tulip
give the embroidery a sense
of depth and perspective.
The gradated threads in the
leaves appear to catch the
light, producing a very
painterly embroidery.*

103

TULIP VARIATION

THIS BRIGHT EMBROIDERY depicts the more formal quality of tulips to great effect; the stiff, neat flowers lined up in simple bands. These different tulip shapes are designed from various silhouettes that are found in modern tulip shapes. The fabric could be used for a number of purposes as it is relatively hardwearing. The choice of bright silks gives the embroidery a lustrous quality.

105

How to work the tulip appliqué

1 Trace the tulips from the image opposite and transfer them onto silk fabric backed with fusible web. **2** Cut the flowers out and press them onto the ground in a half-drop repeat (see page 37). **3** Machine stitch the outlines using a zigzag stitch in contrasting colours to add to the vibrancy of the design.

left: *A formal design suits the elegant simplicity of these tulips, appliquéd in brilliant silks and machine-stitched in place.*

SWEET VIOLET

viola odorata

Simplicity, modesty and faithfulness are the attributes accorded to the violet, a very early spring flower that, in my garden, hides under its handsome evergreen leaves. The sweet scent of the violet is surprisingly strong for such an unassuming little flower. Posies of violets were traditionally sold by flower girls: the inspiration for the embroidery opposite.

above: flower group

This tiny flower is easily embroidered in satin stitches with a single silk thread of the most vibrant purple, which we call violet. The round leaves are worked with satin stitches divided at the centre, and the elegant drooping stems are worked in stem stitch.

106

THE USE OF VELVET for these machine-appliquéd flowers somehow evokes the curious old-fashioned quality of violets. Although I wanted to capture the faded elegance of this flower, the beautiful colour of the living violets made me reach for vibrant silk velvet. The instructions below are for an embroidery on a ground, but for a free-standing flower the leaf can be treated as indicated below and the stems wired as shown on pages 30 and 31.

How to work the three-dimensional sweet violet posy

1 Trace the motifs on page 154. **2** To prevent the velvet fraying, bond it first with fusible web to a finer backing fabric, such as thin habutai silk. (Treated in this way the petals are surprisingly sturdy and will take the normal wear and tear of bought fabric flowers.) **3** Cut and bond the leaf in position on the ground fabric and embroider using a straight machine stitch and space-dyed green and mauve thread. **4** Coax a narrow silk embroidery ribbon in position for the flower stems and straight machine-stitch. **5** Draw each petal separately on the silk-bonded velvet, cut out, assemble to form the flowers and baste. **6** Stretch onto a small hoop and free-motion machine-stitch (see page 23) the centre and stamens using a golden-yellow thread. **7** Stitch a fine satin ribbon bow over the stems to make a posy.

above: *This little posy was inspired by the old-fashioned bunches of violets, tied with straw, and sold in springtime.*

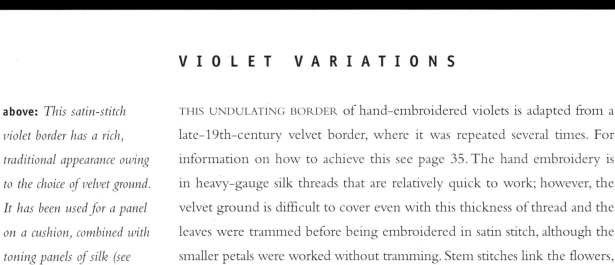

VIOLET VARIATIONS

above: *This satin-stitch violet border has a rich, traditional appearance owing to the choice of velvet ground. It has been used for a panel on a cushion, combined with toning panels of silk (see page 43).*

THIS UNDULATING BORDER of hand-embroidered violets is adapted from a late-19th-century velvet border, where it was repeated several times. For information on how to achieve this see page 35. The hand embroidery is in heavy-gauge silk threads that are relatively quick to work; however, the velvet ground is difficult to cover even with this thickness of thread and the leaves were trammed before being embroidered in satin stitch, although the smaller petals were worked without tramming. Stem stitches link the flowers, and bullion knots have been worked for the centres.

How to work the violet border (above)

1 Take a tracing from the embroidery above and transfer it onto the fabric to be embroidered. (On dark-coloured velvet this can be quite difficult as pen markers will not be visible so the paper transfer system would be advisable, reinforcing the tracing with a chalk outline.) **2** Mount the velvet onto a roller frame stretcher as a hoop would mark the pile and crush the embroidery if it wasn't large enough to take the whole piece of fabric.

How to work the cross-stitch violet (below)

This pretty cross-stitched posy tied with a bow is also an old design which has been stitched onto a dark-coloured counted-thread ground. Three strands of stranded cotton (embroidery floss) have been used for a fine effect. **1** Use the chart on page 147 as the guide for the design. **2** Using three strands in three colours, work the flower. **3** Using two strands of cotton in two greens, work the leaves. **4** Work the bow with two strands in three shades of gold and yellow.

above: *This little violet has been taken from the border opposite, and is worked in long and short stitch and stem stitch with two strands of thread.*

left: *The little cross-stitch violet has been worked on a strongly contrasting ground on an evenweave linen. You could work it on non-counted-thread fabric if you use the waste canvas method shown on page 24.*

109

PANSY

viola tricolor

The name "pansy" is derived from the French word for "thought" (*pensée*). In the language of flowers, pansies symbolize memories. Their jewel-like colours and exceptionally pretty flower faces have long made them popular subjects for embroidery.

above: flower group
This clump of pansies is simply stitched in long and short stitch and satin stitch in bold contrasting colours.

110

opposite: *The realistic nature of these little pansies is achieved by blending the colours. Tramming prior to stitching helps to give the petals definition.*

THIS PRETTY, FLAT-faced flower is one of my favourite flowers to embroider. The range of colours, often combined in extravagant contrasts, allows endless scope for experiment.

For realistic flowers, carefully worked long and short stitches fanned out to follow the growth pattern of each petal allow for the elegant blending of colours. Here the same pansy flower motif has been stitched in a variety of coloured markings, with the addition of different stems, leaves and a bud to give a useful range of information from which to start your own experiments. At least two, but more often three, closely toned versions of each colour will be needed to produce lifelike gradations.

How to work the satin-stitch pansies

1 Copy the motif from page 148 and trace onto the ground fabric using a water-soluble pen. **2** Using two strands of stranded silk (floss), outline each petal in split stitch. **3** Following the growth pattern, satin stitch over the split-stitched outline to cover it. **4** Continue to work any colour blends with two strands, then work over the entire petal with a single strand to define the veins. **5** Tram the stalk with long lengths of thread to give a raised effect and then work in satin stitch. **6** Outline the leaves and bud with the split stitches before working in long and short stitch.

PANSY VARIATIONS

right: *This little three-dimensional pansy would make a beautiful brooch.*

PANSIES LEND THEMSELVES to a range of embroidery styles. Those shown here include a three-dimensional version of the embroidery on the previous page, a graphic image for a napkin and a little cross-stitch pansy: the Victorians loved pansies and many appear in 19th-century cross-stitch pictures.

below: *This cross-stitch pansy has been worked over waste canvas onto a fine linen ground (see page 24).*

112

How to work the hand-embroidered appliquéd pansy (above)

1 Cut the petals and leaf from a selection of wide velvet ribbons, bonded onto a stiff backing. **2** Cut out the shapes before buttonhole stitching the outlines with space-dyed threads through both backing and velvet.

How to work the cross-stitch pansy (left)

1 Transfer the image from page 147 onto counted-thread canvas or waste canvas with a stitch gauge of three per centimetre (eight per inch). Work in four strands of stranded cotton (embroidery floss).

How to work the pansy napkin (right)

1 Trace the motif from page 147. **2** Buttonhole stitch the flower outline, borders and stem. **3** Work the outer centre in stem stitch and the inner centre in satin stitch.

opposite: *The pansy flower, face on, has been applied to a napkin, to add to a set (see pages 142 and 143).*

the stitch glossary

The stitches illustrated here are a very small selection of the great number of stitches available to the embroiderer. Most have been chosen because I use them almost daily in my work. These are the simple line and filling stitches that, when closely and carefully worked in fine threads, enable the embroiderer to describe just about any flower and leaf desired. Other stitches that I often use when designing are those like the lovely herringbone family of crossed stitches which, when repeated, form decorative lines.

All the stitches shown are easy to work but beginners will benefit from some practice. Learning new stitches is one of the early delights of embroidery, as each one can open up a whole new set of ideas and experiments. Ribbon stitch, for example, was new to me: I discovered it while working on this book and immediately saw how it resembled hydrangea flowers, so I used it for that purpose. However, I can imagine that many other flowers could be described with it, by simply changing the colours and the way the flowers are grouped. Crewel work is a delightful way to try new stitch combinations as small sections of the design can be filled in with patterns made by amalgamating several different stitch types. Crewel work provides the perfect introduction to stitches for new embroiderers.

STRAIGHT STITCHES

STRAIGHT STITCHES are the oldest, easiest and most versatile of embroidery stitches. They can be used for both outlining and filling, depending on their configurations and density.

Different effects will be generated according to the type of thread used, but the finest and easiest stitched line is made by using split stitch. It looks like a narrow chain stitch and is perfect for outlining the sinuous curves required for depicting most flowers, whether as a linear embroidery or as an outline for filling stitches. When used for an outline, it is best to overstitch it with the filling stitches to give a more natural effect.

Stem stitch is frequently used as a line stitch and is perfect, as its name implies, for describing any stem, whether straight, curved or crooked, but it is also good for thin leaves. Broken lines made by running or dot stitch are useful to suggest a fading or broken colour, or the elegant trailing off of a stem.

Of the straight stitches used for fillings, the simple and basic satin stitch is most useful for filling small shapes when a flat effect is required; it is also one of the main stitches for the tiny growing plant embroideries on the title pages of the flower directory. The main straight filling stitch is long and short stitch, or for a more even effect, encroaching satin stitch. Both have the facility to blend one shade or colour of yarn into another, as the stitches in one row mesh into the next.

116

Running stitch (below)
This gives a subtle broken line to describe the curve of the convolvulus petals on page 65.

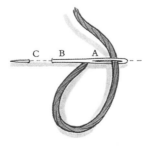

running stitch

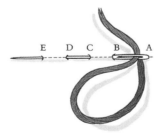

1 *Come up at A, go down at B, then come up at C. Do not pull thread through fabric.*

2 *Go down at D, and come up at E. Pull thread through gently so fabric does not pucker.*

3 *Continue following design line as shown by repeating steps 1 and 2. Keep stitches even.*

stem stitch

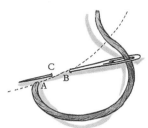

1 *Come up at A, go down at B, then come up at C above working thread. Pull thread through.*

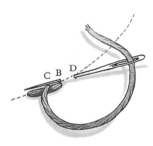

2 *Keeping thread below needle, go down at D and come up at B to complete second stitch.*

3 *Repeat Step 2 to continue stitching along row as shown, keeping stitches evenly sized.*

Stem stitch (above)
Here it is used to depict both the stalks and narrow leaves of lavender in two threads of stranded cotton (embroidery floss) as seen on page 83.

Backstitch (below)
This is ideal for making simple stems in naïve embroideries, such as the daisy border on page 61, worked in a medium-weight glossy pearl cotton.

backstitch

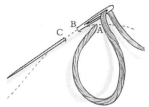

1 *Working from right to left, come up at A, go down at B, then come up at C. Pull thread through.*

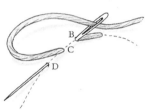

2 *Go down again at B to make a backstitch, then come up at D, ready for the next stitch.*

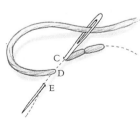

3 *Pull thread through, go down at C and come up at E. Repeat as above to work a backstitched line.*

1 1 7

Straight stitch (right)
This is perfect for capturing the natural qualities of the simple daisy flowers when the stitch lengths are varied using two strands of stranded cotton (embroidery floss) as in the small embroidery on page 60.

straight (stroke) stitch

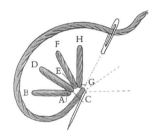

1 To create a straight-stitch fan, come up at A, go down at B, and up at C. Repeat, going down at D, up at E, down at F, up at G, and down at H.

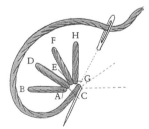

2 Continue working in this way until you have worked a half-circle of evenly spaced stitches. Secure thread at back of work.

118

Satin stitch (below)
This is best used in a glossy heavy thread that reflects light when densely stitched, such as on the little violet flowers on page 109.

satin stitch

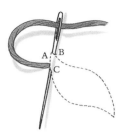

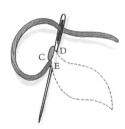

1 Come up at A, go down at B, and come up at C. Pull thread through gently ready for next stitch.

2 Placing stitches close together, go down at D and come up at E. Follow exact guidelines of motif for even edge.

3 Continue in this manner to fill motif, keeping an even tension so that the surface remains smooth.

Encroaching satin stitch (above)

This is a good method for controlling the blending of colours when using a shaded thread, as the uniformity of the stitches makes the gradual colour change apparent. The slanted variation shown here (from the tulip on page 103) makes it easier to describe the shading of the undulating leaf and gives a feeling of upward growth.

encroaching satin stitch

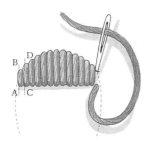 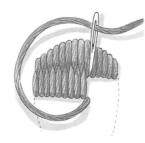

1 Working from left to right, come up at A, go down at B (at edge of motif), up at C, and down at D. Continue to complete row 1.

2 To work similar band of stitches, insert needle between and just above base of two corresponding stitches on previous row. Keep stitches even.

Split stitch (right)

This is a perfect outlining stitch and especially good for decorative patterning in crewel work (see page 62).

split stitch

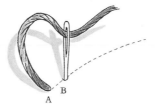 

1 Come up at A and go down at B, forming a straight stitch on outline of motif. Pull thread through.

2 Come up at C (just short of halfway between A and B), piercing thread of previous stitch.

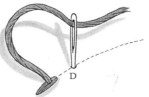

3 Pull thread through and go down at D, to form next stitch, following outline of motif.

4 Repeat Steps 2 and 3, continuing to pierce last stitch worked. Pull thread through gently; do not break thread fibres.

119

5 When row is complete, work a final straight stitch, taking thread to back of fabric, and secure.

long and short stitch

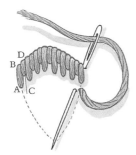

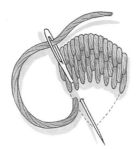

1 *Come up at A, go down at B, up at C, and down at D. Continue alternating long and short stitches across row from left to right.*

2 *Repeat, this time working long stitches only across row to fill motif. The last row will require some short stitches.*

Raised satin stitch (above)

This is an evenly worked straight stitch over a bed of other straight stitches. Also called tramming, this technique prevents the ground fabric from showing through, making it useful for stitching light colours onto a dark ground (see violets on page 108).

raised satin stitch

Long and short stitch (above)

As its name implies, this is a straight stitch worked in various lengths, making it possible to blend one row of stitches with the next when infilling a shape, such as a petal. This makes it easy to merge colours imperceptibly (see the pansies on page 111).

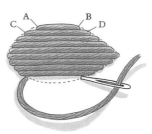

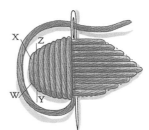

1 *Come up at A, go down at B, up at C, and down at D. Continue to fill motif with evenly worked basic satin stitch.*

2 *Come up at W, go down at X, up at Y, and down at Z. Continue until base stitches are completely covered.*

darning stitch

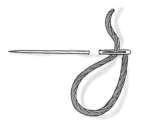

1 *First weave needle in and out of fabric to create single row of horizontal straight stitches. Work from right to left, and keep stitching even.*

2 *To make evenly sized and spaced rows as shown, continue working back and forth along area to be filled, until pattern is complete.*

Fern stitch (above)

This is a pretty stitch that perfectly describes a fern frond, especially when it is worked so that the upward strokes of the stitch are gradated and develop into a scroll at the tip using split or small stem stitches (see pages 114-5).

fern stitch

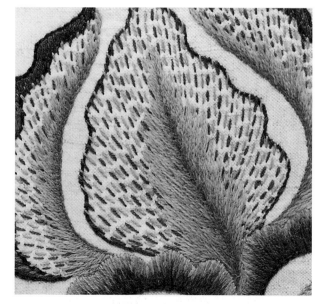

Darning stitch (above)

This is a uniform version of running stitch and has been used here as a way of blending in two colours decoratively on a neutral ground for crewel work (see page 81). It is often used in more decorative patterns by varying the lengths of the stitches.

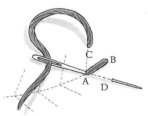

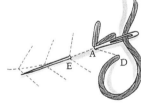

1 *Come up at A on central stem of design. Go down at B, then come up at C, go back down at A, and come up at D as shown.*

2 *Go down at A again and up at E on centre guideline, ready for next group of stitches. Repeat from B in Step 1.*

seed stitch

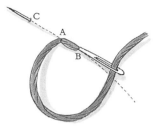

1 *Come up at A and go down at B. Come up again where you want next stitch to start.*

2 *Work stitches at random angles, as shown here, to fill in design shape or background area.*

dot stitch

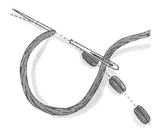

1 *Come up at A, and go down at B. Come up again at A and down again at B, then come up at C.*

2 *Work in an evenly spaced line to create a dotted-line effect, or place dots at random.*

Seed stitch (above)
This is worked randomly in a heavy-gauge thread at the centre of the hellebore flower on page 74, where it suggests the heavy dots of pollen surrounding the tightly packed stamens.

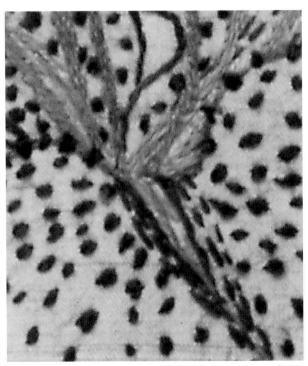

Dot stitch (above)
Used to describe the speckled and spotted markings on the lily petals on page 87, the direction of the straight rows of dots from the central line helps to suggest the curve of the petals.

LOOPED STITCHES

LOOPED STITCHES are usually one of the first embroidery stitches that we are taught as children, both "lazy daisy" and chain stitches belonging to the loop stitch family. Single or detached chain stitch, apart from its likeness to single petals, bears a remarkable resemblance to lavender florets and, if you group the stitches together in rows, you can easily capture the likeness of a lavender spike.

The likeness of looped stitches to petals is also reflected in petal chain stitch, which is a continuous row of straight and chain stitches; it is decorative enough to act as a border in place of a braid or lace when edging another embroidery. The decorative likeness that stitches have to different natural forms is reflected in the traditional names given to variations of the looped stitch family: wheatear, feather, double feather and feathered chain stitches are seen on many traditional European embroideries, but most notably in crewel work and on English smocks, where rows of these stitches border the smocking patterns.

However, the most useful and commonly used stitch is blanket stitch or its closed-up variation, buttonhole stitch. The latter, stitched closely together, prevents a raw edge from fraying. It can also be used to describe a wide line, the width of which can be varied by controlling the length of the upward stroke of the stitch. The effect of this wide line is attractively naive and so simple that a child could easily master it.

Blanket stitch (below)
This is the wider spaced variation of buttonhole stitch and it is seen here as a decorative crewel-work stitch on a leaf (depicted on the curtain on pages 48 and 49).

123

buttonhole (blanket) stitch

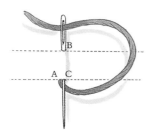

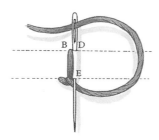

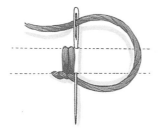

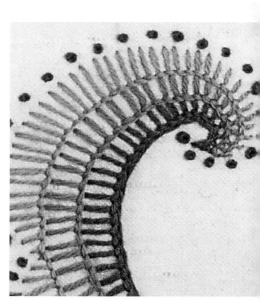

1 *Come up at A and go down at B, and come up at C, just to immediate right of A. Carry thread under needle point from left to right. Pull thread through.*

2 *Go down at D (just to immediate right of B). Come up at E, keeping thread under needle point.*

3 *Continue in this way along row, keeping all stitches even and close together as shown.*

chain & detached chain stitch

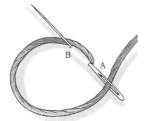

1 *Make a looped stitch by inserting the needle at A, looping the thread counter-clockwise to the left of the needle and coming up within the loop at B.*

2 *Make a similar stitch, going down at B and coming up at C, and so on.*

Detached chain stitch:
Work a detached stitch by repeating Step 1. Pull through and make a small stitch to anchor loop. Work five detached stitches in a circle to create lazy daisy stitch.

124

Chain stitches (above)
These are worked in groups of two colours to suggest the florets of lavender depicted on page 83 and on the apron on page 44.

Feather stitch (below)
This is a decorative stitch traditionally seen in all types of early embroidery, useful for filling in odd shapes for crewel work.

feather stitch

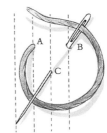

1 *Come up at A, go down at B, and come up at C. Carry thread under needle point from left to right.*

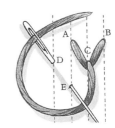

2 *Take needle to left of C, go down at D, and come up at E. Carry thread under needle point from left to right.*

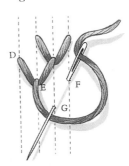

3 *Continue in this way, going down at F, coming up at G. Carry thread under needle point from left to right.*

Double feather stitch (above)

This is a variation on feather stitch (opposite) and has been used to decorative effect on the curtains on pages 48 and 49.

double feather stitch

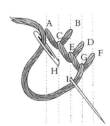 

1 *Come up at A, down at B, and come up at C, keeping needle over stitch just made. Repeat, following letter sequence. Then cross to left, go down at H and up at I.*

2 *Repeat, going down at J, up at K, down at L, up at M, down at N, up at O. Continue working two stitches to left and two to right, keeping loops even.*

feathered chain

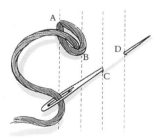 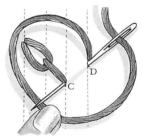

1 *Come up at A. Make a loop and go down next to A, coming up through loop at B. Slant to the right, go down at C, and come up at D.*

2 *Pull thread through. Go down next to D, then come up at C. Loop thread under point of needle and pull thread through gently.*

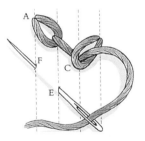 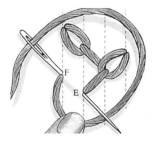

3 *Go down at E and then come up at F (below A) as shown to make a straight stitch. Pull thread through.*

4 *Go down next to F and come up at E, keeping thread under point of needle. Pull thread through.*

125

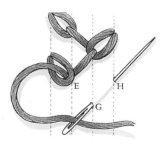

5 *Go down at G and come up at H. Repeat from Step 2 to continue the column, following guide lines.*

petal stitch

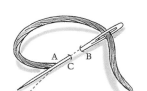

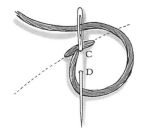

1 *Come up at A, go down at B, and up at C, following guide line and keeping thread to the left as shown.*

2 *Pull thread through. Go down next to C and come up at D with working thread under needle to create loop.*

126

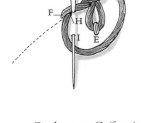

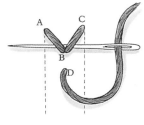

3 *Pull thread through and go down at E making a small stitch to secure loop. Come up at F.*

4 *Go down at G (forming stem stitch); come up at H. Pull through. Go down next to H and up at I as shown.*

Petal stitch (above, top)

This is a combination of two stitches, feather and chain, and has long been a popular, traditional, decorative embroidery stitch. Looking like a small-leafed branch, it lends itself perfectly as a filling pattern for larger crewel-work leaves, which you can see in more detail on page 46.

wheatear stitch

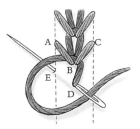

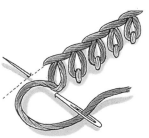

5 *Repeat from Step 3 to form a line of stitches. Work carefully to keep stitching even.*

1 *Come up at A, go down at B, up at C, down at B again, up at D. Without picking up fabric, slide needle from right to left through bottom of the V just made.*

2 *Go down at D and then come up at E, ready for next stitch. Repeat from Step 1 to continue working column of stitches as desired.*

cretan stitch

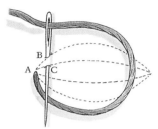 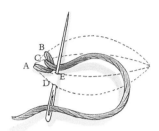 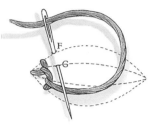 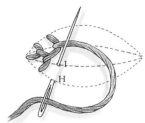

1 *Come up at A, go down at B, and up at C, keeping working thread under needle point.*

2 *Go down at D, following motif outline, and come up at E, keeping working thread under needle.*

3 *Go down a short distance along F, coming up at G with thread under needle point as shown.*

4 *Go down at H and then come up at I, again keeping thread under needle point as shown.*

127

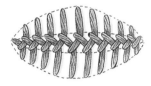

5 *Continue in this way. Vary size of stitch by extending or shortening the central crossover.*

Cretan stitch (right, below) This is a decorative filling stitch, perfect for working small leaves on a naïve embroidery, such as the daisy border shown on page 61, where it has been outlined in back stitch. It also makes a wide line that can be gradated to look like a fern frond.

CROSSED STITCHES

CROSS STITCH must be the most popular stitch for decorative purposes today; it is often used almost as an embroiderer's "painting by numbers" technique, and counted cross stitch ensures pleasing results when worked from charts onto evenweave fabrics. There is no need to restrict the choice of fabric grounds as there is an evenweave canvas available, called waste canvas, which is designed to be placed on a plain fabric as a guide for the stitches and then pulled away once the stitching is complete.

There are many interesting decorative versions within the cross-stitch family and they are easy and pleasurable to work. The basic rule of all crossed stitches is that the top stitches should all cross in the same direction, which ensures an even and uniformly textured surface to the work. Star stitch is a large and decorative stitch resembling small daisies and is useful for describing many multi-flowered plants, its combination of two different crosses enabling it to be made of different colours and quality of threads, always an advantage when capturing the subtlety of flower textures.

Herringbone stitch is an elegant linear stitch made from a series of long-armed cross stitches. It is perfect for adding rows of decorative patterns and is very useful when designing, as there are many variations that can carry different coloured threads to make harmonious colour variations. Used with straight stitches that extend over the outer crosses or running stitches to weave in and out of the inner crosses, variations and embellishments are easily achieved.

128

Cross stitch (below)
This makes a neat square shape of solid but textured colour that can be built up into designs, such as the tiny violets seen on page 109.

cross stitch

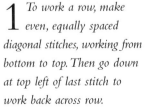

Single cross stitch:
Come up at A, down at B, up at C, down at D. The stitch can be reversed so that the top half slants from lower right to upper left.

1 *To work a row, make even, equally spaced diagonal stitches, working from bottom to top. Then go down at top left of last stitch to work back across row.*

2 *Continue in same manner, slanting stitches in opposite direction to form a row of crosses.*

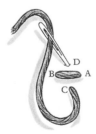

Star filling stitch (left)
This perfectly describes the allium flowers on page 55, as it can be worked in two different colours to capture the lively colour combinations of the different plant forms, but it would be useful for any other starry-flowered plant.

star filling stitch

1 *Work a single St George's cross stitch (see below), stitching from A to B, then from C to D as shown.*

2 *Come up at E and go down at F, working a diagonal stitch of equal length across middle of first cross.*

3 *Come up at G and then go down at H to complete second cross, again keeping stitch equal in length.*

4 *To begin first half of the small inner cross, come up at I and then go down at J as shown.*

5 *Come up at K and go down at L to complete small cross, keeping K-L the same length as I-J.*

St George's cross stitch
(below)
This version of cross stitch has been used to tie down the threads of Jacobean laidwork on the fritillary on page 73.

129

St George's cross stitch

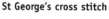

1 *To work a single cross, come up at A, go down at B, come up at C, and go down at D as shown.*

2 *To create a row, work a line of evenly spaced horizontal stitches. Then cross each with a same-sized vertical stitch.*

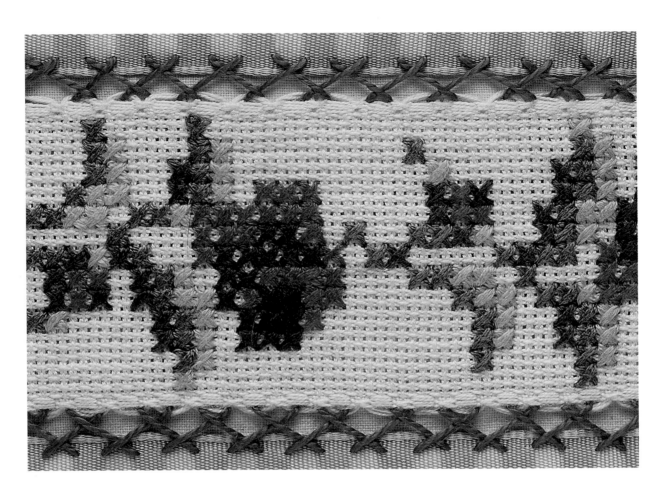

herringbone stitch

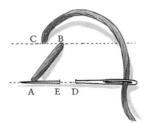

1 *Come up at A, go down at B, come up at C. Cross down and insert at D, coming up at E. Threads will cross at top.*

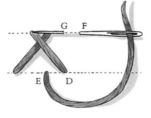

2 *Cross up and insert at F, then come up at G. Pull through. Threads will cross at bottom.*

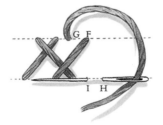

3 *Cross down and insert at H, coming up at I. Continue along row by repeating steps 1 and 2.*

Herringbone stitch (above) This is a linear crossed stitch that can be embellished with many other stitches. However, seen here in its basic form, it is used as a decorative functional stitch to hold down the edges of the ribbon on the pillow projects on page 47.

KNOTTED STITCHES

ALTHOUGH NOT many knotted stitches have been used in this book, they are vital because they so closely resemble seeds, pollen heads or tiny buds. Knotted stitches can be worked on any fine fabrics but individual knots need to be worked over an intersection of threads, otherwise the knot will be pulled through to the back of the fabric.

Practice is needed to create evenly sized knots, as they require the thread to be wrapped several times around the needle and the free hand is needed to both ease the needle through the complete stitch while holding it simultaneously in place next to the ground fabric, and so preventing the knot from travelling up the thread. It is necessary for the ground fabric to be stretched taut to enable the knots to be stitched easily, for which a hoop or frame is necessary.

A perfectly formed knot looks like a small round bead, but uniformity is not always required for creating naturalist effects in an embroidery, so you can use a variety of windings to create differently sized knots for buds and seeds.

French knots are the basic stitch used throughout the book, but the bullion knot, an elongated rolled knot, while a little more difficult to work, has many applications. When worked in groups of small circles, bullion knots look uncannily like miniature full-blown roses; by using closely toned shades of thread, subtle variations of colour can be achieved.

French knots (below)
These are useful and easy knots to use for all types of seeds and tiny buds. They are shown here as the florets of the lace-cap hydrangea on page 79.

131

french knot

1 *Come up at A and wrap thread around needle once in counter-clockwise direction.*

2 *Wrap thread around needle a second time in same direction, keeping needle away from fabric.*

3 *Push wraps together and slide to end of needle. Go down close to starting point, pulling thread through to form a knot.*

bullion knot

1 *Come up at A, go down at B, and back up at A, as though forming a back-stitch. Do not pull needle through.*

2 *Wind thread around needle point until a length equal to or greater than the distance between A and B is covered.*

3 *Hold down coiled threads with finger and pull needle gently through. Be careful not to distort coil by pulling thread too hard.*

4 *The stitch now resembles a coiled cord. Bring needle to right to move coil in place between A and B. Pull extra thread through coil to take up slack.*

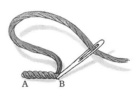

5 *Go down at B again to anchor stitch in place. If coil is longer than A-B, coil will be raised on fabric surface, giving a three-dimensional effect.*

Bullion knot (left)
This is an elongated knot which, when worked in semi-circles in two shades of a colour to give depth, makes the prettiest roses. They are shown here covering the elegant standard bush rose on page 99.

Basic couching (left)
This is shown here with the stitches of the second thread worked in a direction that follows the twist of the laid or couched thread, making it easier to turn curves with the first thread and so suggesting the curvaceous stamens of the crewel-work pinks on page 71.

COUCHING STITCHES

COUCHING IS THE TERM given to laying down one thread and oversewing it with another thread. Couching has two main uses: as a fine, raised outlining or detailing thread or as a decorative surface treatment.

Basic couching gives the finest line of any surface stitch; it is as fine as the available thread and has been used in the Floral Directory for the finest tendrils, stamens and stalks. Whipped stem stitch, although not strictly a couching stitch, shares a similar function: it is really for giving linear embroidery some extra texture or coaxing it into a more fluid line. Satin couching is a raised stitch that looks rather like bullion knots, but long lengths can be embroidered for ridged and textured surfaces.

Decorative couching can be made by using many different stitches in the Stitch Glossary to hold down other materials. Cross-stitch couching has been used to attach narrow ribbons with different coloured thread; using two different yarns or colours offers exciting possibilities for sampling a host of different decorative ideas.

The traditional decorative couching technique is Jacobean laidwork, which is found in most crewel-work designs. The two layers of laid threads are crossed to make a trellis effect, which is then stitched in position with either a single diagonal stitch or crossed stitches. This simple trellis can be adapted to include many other stitches to add to the overall decorative effect. French knots can be placed between the trellis spaces, longer straight stitches can pass over two threads to create tartan-type patterns and other different formations of diamond and square trellises can be arranged. Cloud filling stitch looks rather like Jacobean laidwork but is worked in reverse with the small, straight stitches worked before being threaded with a second yarn producing a softer effect than usual couching.

133

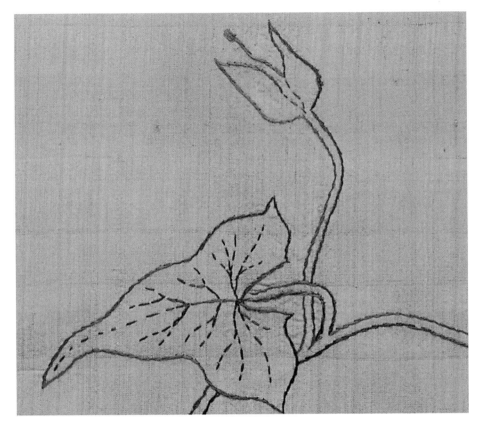

Basic couching (left)
This is used here as the finest line in the stamen on the convolvulus plant on pages 64-5. It is made of one single laid strand of stranded silk (embroidery floss), couched down with an even finer sewing silk. Basic couching is also a useful means of stitching with a heavy thread that would damage the ground fabric if it were stitched through it in the normal manner.

basic couching

1 Thread a large-eyed needle with the thread to be couched and bring it through the fabric at A. Take the thread back through fabric at end of desired line length.

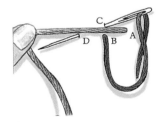

2 Using fine couching thread, come up at B; go down at C, covering laid thread; and come up at D.

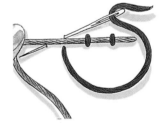

3 Repeat along row, holding and controlling the laid line with fingers of other hand.

satin couching

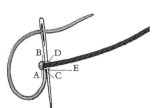 

1 *Lay down the first thread. Bring the contrasting couching thread up at A. Go down at B, directly above laid thread, come up next to A at C. Go down at D, next to B, come up at E as shown.*

2 *Continue working in this way until the laid thread is completely covered and cannot be seen under the couched threads. Pack the stitches tightly and evenly together, keeping the edges regular.*

cross-stitch couching

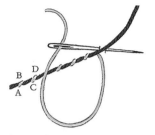 

1 *Lay down the first thread. Bring the contrasting couching thread up at A and make a slanted crossing stitch, going down at B, up at C, down at D, and so on to complete the row of slanted stitches.*

2 *When row is complete, work from the other end of the row, still using the same thread. Come up at A, go down at B, up at C, down at D, and so on, slanting stitches over those already worked to form crosses.*

135

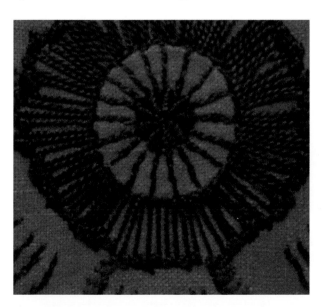

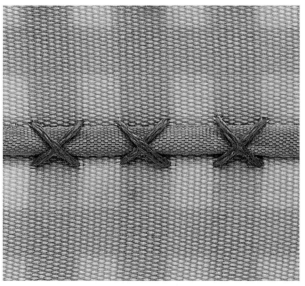

Satin couching (above)
This has been used in short lengths radiating out over a base of straight stitches to form the central boss of a poppy seedhead. Stitched in pearl cotton it forms strong ridges (see page 93).

Cross-stitch couching (above)
This has been used on the pillow project on page 47 as a decorative means of holding down a narrow ribbon on a wider gingham ribbon, and allows contrasting colours to be introduced.

jacobean laidwork

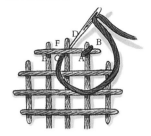

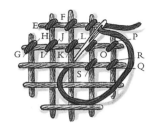

1 *Fill the motif with single, parallel, vertical stitches as shown, working from top to bottom, bottom to top.*

2 *Work long horizontal stitches over the vertical stitches to form a grid. Work from left to right, right to left.*

3 *Using a contrasting thread, come up at A, go down at B, up at C, down at D, and up at E. Go down at F.*

4 *Come up at G, go down at H. Continue back and forth across motif, following letter sequence.*

136

5 *Repeat Step 3, working diagonal stitches in opposite direction to form crosses and complete the trellis effect.*

Jacobean laidwork (right)
This has been worked in two different coloured threads to form the distinctive decorative lattice patterns so typical of traditional crewel-work designs (seen here in a detail from the curtain on pages 48 and 49).

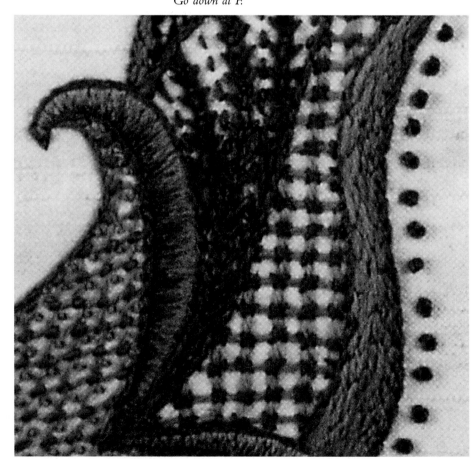

cloud filling stitch

1 *Work rows of evenly spaced, small vertical stitches. Come up to right of A, carry thread through vertical stitches (B, C and D), and go down under E. Do not pick up background fabric.*

2 *Come up at F, weaving up through E, down through G, up through C and so on. Continue working back and forth across each row.*

Whipped stem stitch (above)

The "whipping" thread is almost imperceptible when worked with self-coloured thread to strengthen the line of a curving stem as it turns towards a leaf (see page 87).

whipped stem stitch

1 *Work a foundation row of stem stitch (see page 117) with your base thread, following the motif outline.*

2 *With a contrasting thread, whip thread over and under each stitch in row. Do not pick up background fabric.*

Cloud filling stitch (above)

This makes the traditional honeycomb pattern so often used for the decorative infilling of leaf shapes on crewel work (as shown on page 49).

RIBBON STITCHES

THESE STITCHES are useful, but do not fit into any traditional stitch category, so I have grouped them together here. Ribbon embroidery has been fashionable for some time now and you can buy a good selection of special narrow ribbons that are particularly attractive to work with (see page 13). The first stitch shown, ribbon stitch, makes perfect petals when used with wider ribbons in soft shaded colours. Many different flowers can be depicted depending on the colours used and the formations of the individual stitches. The other ribbon stitch, spider web rose stitch, is really charming and very easy to work, especially if several shades of one colour are used. Combined with longer ribbon stitches in different greens, the spider web rose stitch is very useful for creating realistic-looking leaves.

Ribbon stitch (below)
This stitch perfectly captures the fading blues of the hydrangea flowers depicted on page 79.

ribbon stitch

138

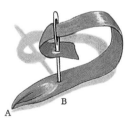

1 *With ribbon locked in needle head, come up at A, and go down at B through ribbon and fabric.*

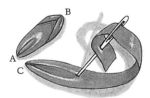

2 *Pull ribbon through loosely and come up at C, ready to begin next stitch. Repeat steps to form a flower head shape.*

Spider web rose stitch (left)
This gives a pretty,
old-fashioned charm to ribbon
work. The use of different
shaded ribbons gives subtlety
and depth to the embroidered
ribbon band (see page 100).

spider web rose

139

1 *Work a straight stitch
(see page 118) with
pearl or stranded cotton
(embroidery floss).*

2 *Work four additional
straight stitches, radiating
from a central point.*

3 *When web is complete,
lock ribbon in needle
(shown opposite) and come
up through fabric at A.*

4 *Weave ribbon over and
under straight stitches as
shown without entering
background fabric.*

5 *Continue working
outward, keeping ribbons
loose until "web" is covered.
Take needle and ribbon
through fabric and secure.*

motifs

This section of the book provides those flower patterns that are not easily traced directly from the flowers in the Floral Directory and those that involve fabric overlays for appliqués or charts. All the motifs are designed to be used in conjunction with the information for embroidering each flower that accompanies the illustrations in the directory. For reasons of space, many of the flowers have been reduced; the reduction size is given so that you can resize them using a photocopier or using the method on page 19. The flowers worked on neutral fabrics in the directory are all reproduced at the size they were embroidered. Where motifs are given in outline, you can select different techniques from those chosen if you wish; the large, simple, buttonhole-stitch designs could easily be stitched using crewel-work patterns, for example. Conversely, the crewel-work designs could make interesting machine-stitched appliqués, as could the pansies and tulips. The directional dotted lines shown on the tulip, iris and pansy motifs are the stitch directions, and need to be copied with a water-soluble pen onto any fabric that is to be embroidered. Any other dotted lines appearing on the motifs are indications of petal overlays for appliqué patterns. The hand-embroidered poppy appliqué requires two layers of fabric so both patterns are given for one petal, together with the information required to join them.

BUTTONHOLE-STITCH FLOWERS

1 Convolvulus *35% size* (see page 67)

2 Anemone *35% size* (see page 59)

3 Poppy *35% size* (see page 93)

4 Auricula *35% size* (see page 96)

5 Pansy *35% size* (see page 113)

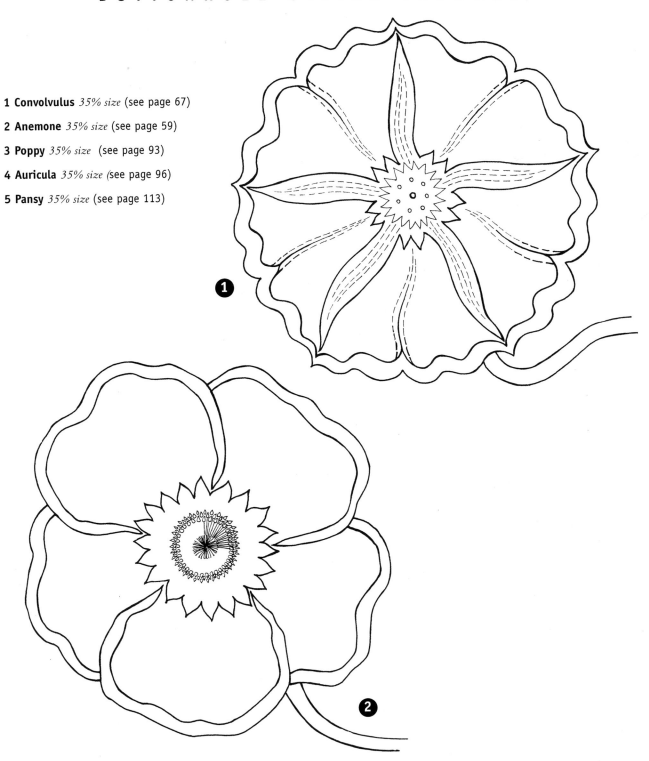

CREWEL WORK

1 Iris *50% size* (see page 81)

2 Cornflower *50% size* (see page 62)

3 Leaf *50% size* (see pages 48 and 49)

4 Pinks *50% size* (see page 71)

144

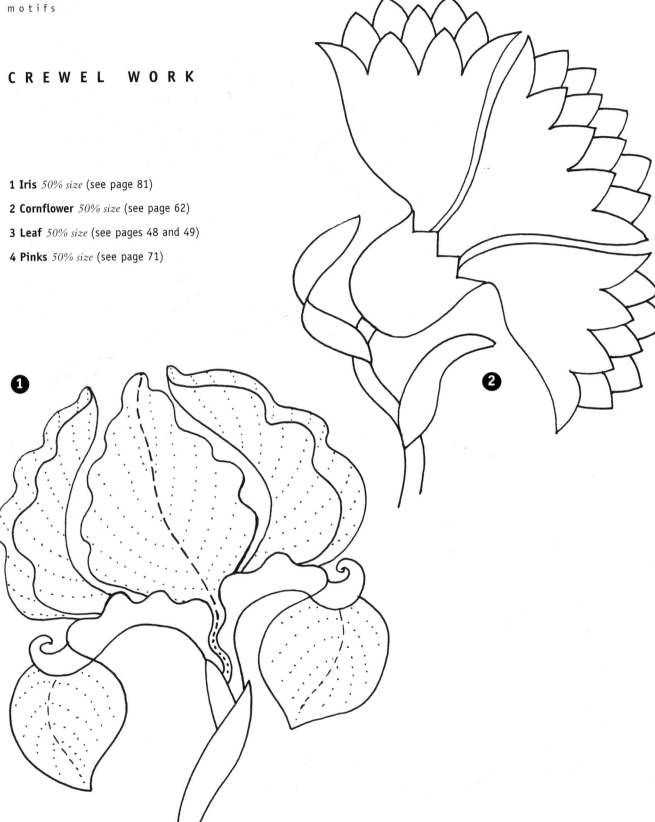

CROSS-STITCH CHARTS

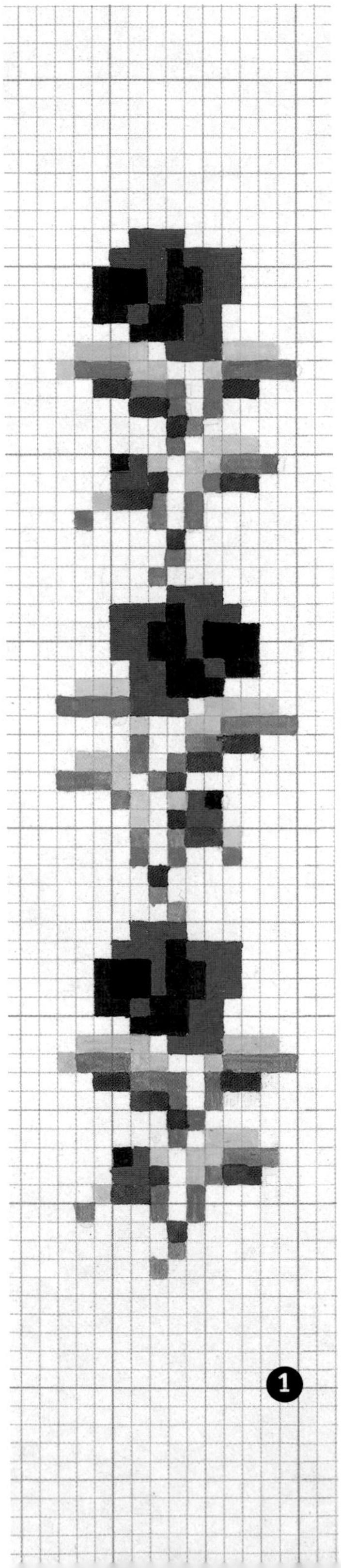

146

1

2

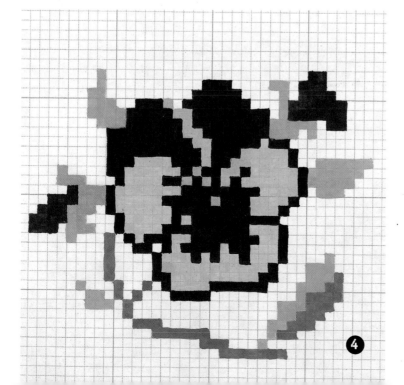

1 Rose border (see page 100)

2 Pinks (see page 69)

3 Rose (see page 98)

4 Pansy (see page 112)

5 Violet (see page 109)

STITCH DIRECTIONS

148

4

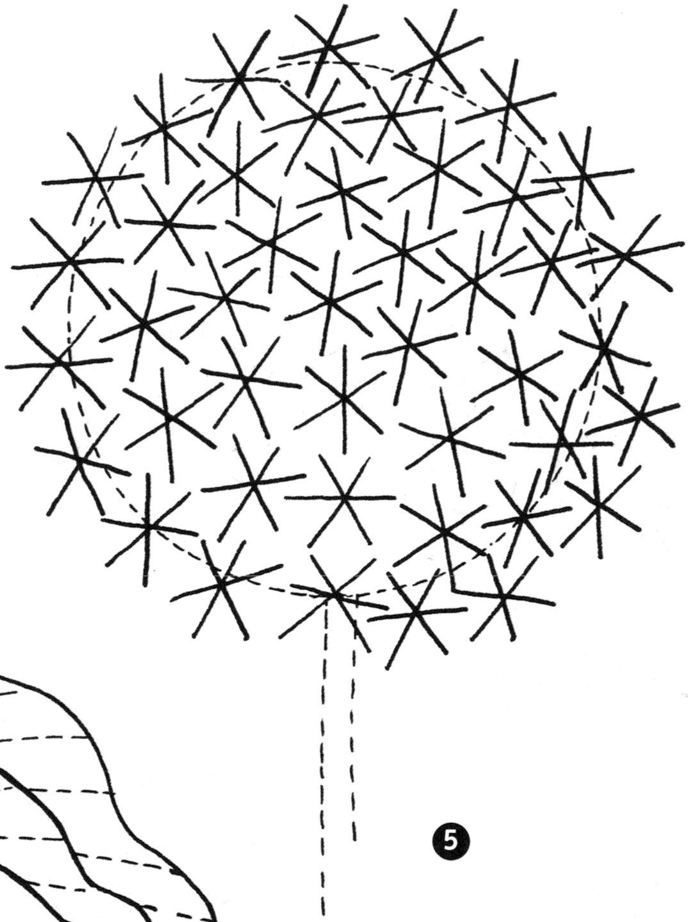

5

149

1 Rose *50% size* (see page 101)

2 Hydrangea *50% size* (see page 79)

3 Pansy *100% size* (see page 111)

4 Tulip *100% size* (see page 103)

5 Allium *100% size* (see page 55)

MISCELLANEOUS PATTERNS

150

1 Auricula *70% size* (see page 95) Cut six

flowers, rings and circles, plus two leaves.

2 Pansy *70% size* (see page 112)

Dotted lines indicate overlap of petals.

3 Anemones *70% size* (see page 57)

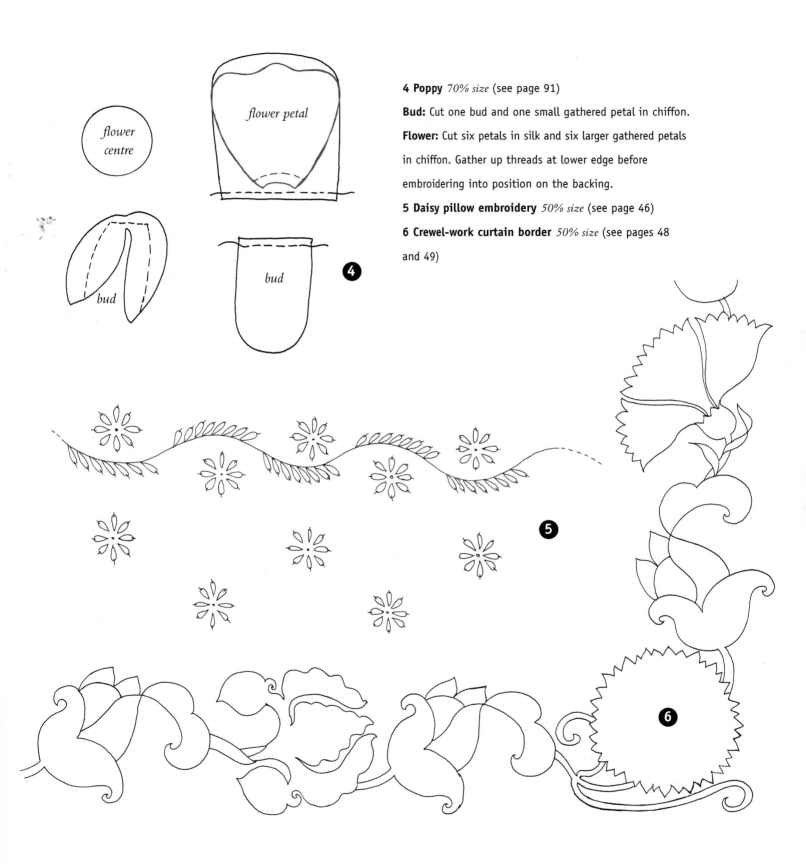

flower centre

flower petal

bud

bud

4 Poppy *70% size* (see page 91)

Bud: Cut one bud and one small gathered petal in chiffon.

Flower: Cut six petals in silk and six larger gathered petals in chiffon. Gather up threads at lower edge before embroidering into position on the backing.

5 Daisy pillow embroidery *50% size* (see page 46)

6 Crewel-work curtain border *50% size* (see pages 48 and 49)

HAND AND MACHINE EMBROIDERY

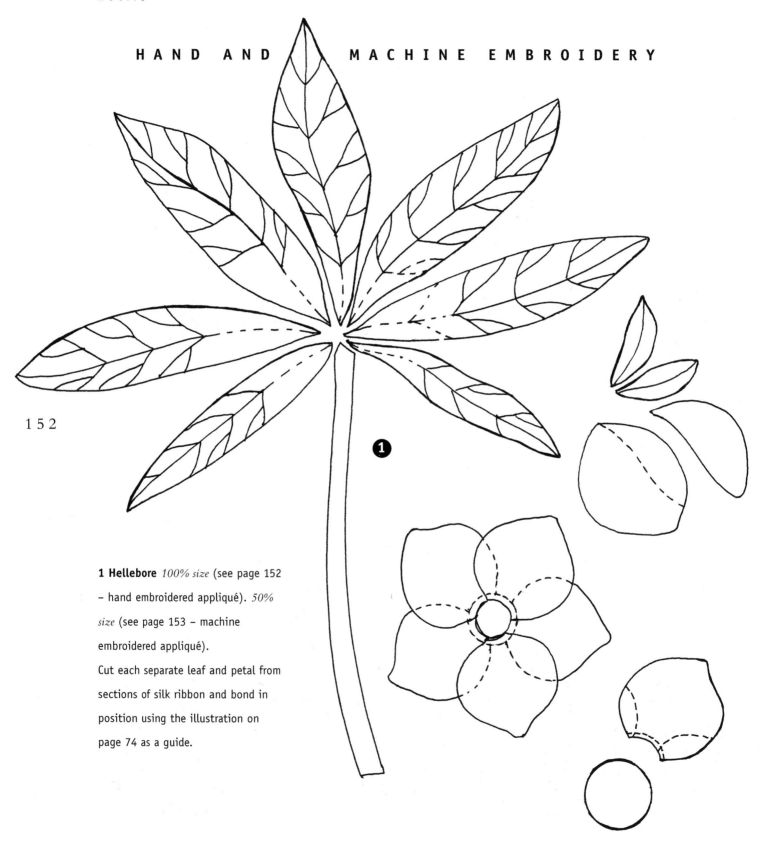

152

1 Hellebore *100% size* (see page 152 – hand embroidered appliqué). *50% size* (see page 153 – machine embroidered appliqué).

Cut each separate leaf and petal from sections of silk ribbon and bond in position using the illustration on page 74 as a guide.

MACHINE EMBROIDERY

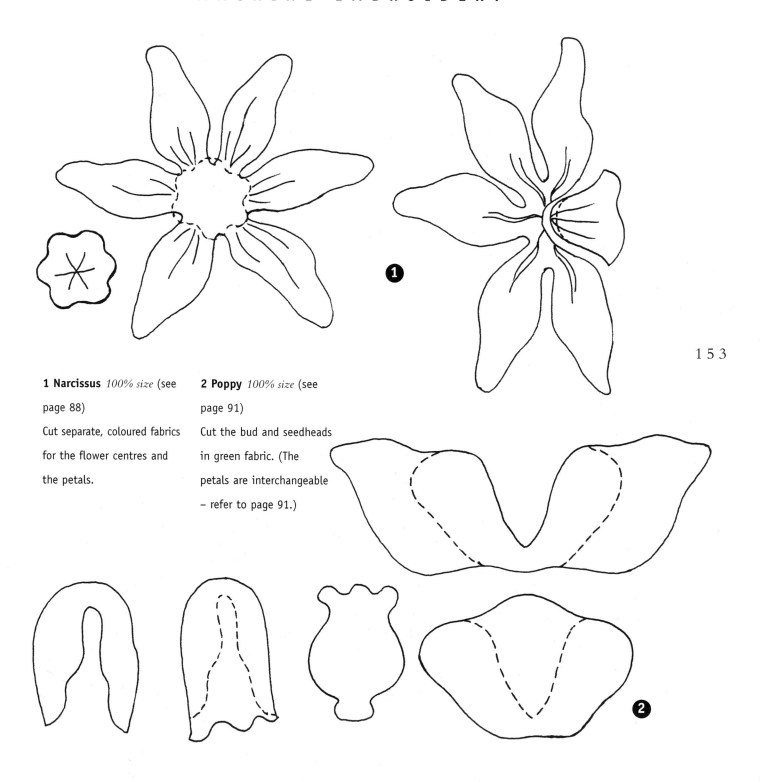

1 Narcissus *100% size* (see page 88)
Cut separate, coloured fabrics for the flower centres and the petals.

2 Poppy *100% size* (see page 91)
Cut the bud and seedheads in green fabric. (The petals are interchangeable – refer to page 91.)

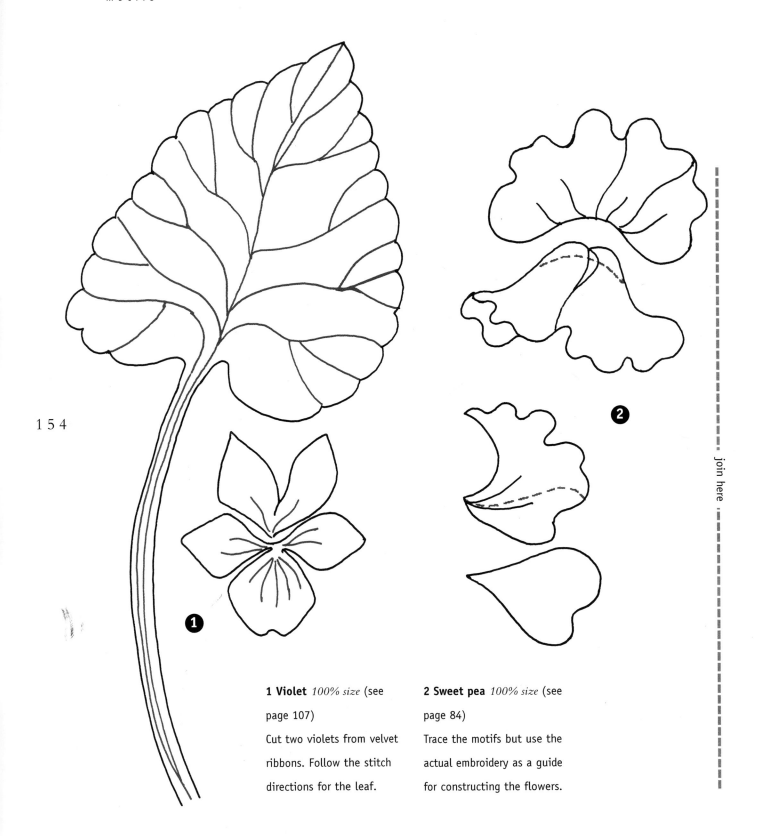

join here

1 Violet *100% size* (see page 107)
Cut two violets from velvet ribbons. Follow the stitch directions for the leaf.

2 Sweet pea *100% size* (see page 84)
Trace the motifs but use the actual embroidery as a guide for constructing the flowers.

join here

155

SUPPLIERS

Anchor:

Stranded cottons (floss) and pearl cottons in solid and space-dyed colours, and tapestry wool yarns

Coats Crafts (UK)
PO Box 22, The Lingfield Estate,
McMullen Road, Darlington,
Co. Durham DL1 1YQ
Tel 01325 365457

Coats and Clark (USA)
4135 South Stream Blvd, Charlotte,
N. Carolina 28217
Tel (704) 329 5016

For tapestry- and crewel-wool yarns

Appleton Bros Ltd
Church Street, Chiswick,
London W4 2PE
Tel 020 8994 0711

Au Ver a Soie:

Stranded silk thread (floss) and silk pearl in solid colours

The Silver Thimble (UK)
The Old Malthouse, Clarence Street,
Bath BA1 5NS
Tel (01225) 423457

Access Commodities Inc (USA)
PO Box 1355, 1129 S Virginia Street,
Terrell, Texas 75160
Tel (972) 563 3313

The Caron Collection

Space-dyed multi-coloured threads; stranded silks and cottons (floss), single strand and 3-ply cotton

Macleod Craft Marketing (UK)
West Yonderton, Warlock Road,
Bridge of Weir PA11 3SR
Tel 01505 612618

Macleod Craft Marketing (USA)
55 Old South Avenue, Stratford,
CT 06497
Tel (203) 381 9999

DMC:

For stranded cottons in solid and space-dyed colours, tapestry- and fine crewel-wool yarns and waste canvas

DMC Creative World Ltd (UK)
Pullman Road, Wigston, Leicestershire
LE18 2DY
Tel (0116) 281 1040

DMC Corporation (USA)
Building 10, Port Kearney, New Jersey
Tel (201) 589 0606

Ribbons· in silk, velvet, georgette, rayon, – space-dyed and hand-dyed in every imaginable combination

Nostalgia (UK)
147A Nottingham Road, Eastwood,
Nottingham NG16 3GJ

Other ribbons

Hanah Silk (USA)
310 Beloit Avenue, Los Angeles
CA 90049

Ruban et Fleur (USA)
8655 S Sepulveda Blvd, Los Angeles
CA 90045

156

INDEX

BIBLIOGRAPHY

The Embroiderers' Flowers

Thomasina Beck

(David and Charles) 1992

ISBN 0 7153 9901 2

Bloom

Li Edelkoort

(Flammarion Press) 2001

ISBN 2 080 10 623 6

The Language of Flowers

Margaret Pickston

(Michael Joseph) 1968

ISBN 0 7181 0593 1

The Florilegium of Alexander Marshall

Prudence Leith-Ross

(RHS Enterprises Ltd) 2000

ISBN 1 902 163 05 2

Picturing Plants

Gill Saunders

(University Press of California)

ISBN 0-520-203062

Annuals and Biennials

Roger Phillips and Martin Rix

(Macmillan) 1999

ISBN 0 333 748 891

Perennials, Early

Phillips and Rix

(Macmillan) 1991

ISBN 0 330 32774 7

Perennials, Late

Phillips and Rix

(Macmillan) 1991

ISBN 0 330 32775 5

Bulbs

Phillips and Rix

(Pan) 1981

ISBN 0 330 30253 1

acknowledgments I want to thank the following people who worked with me to produce this book so that it reflects the delight I find in embroidering and designing with flowers. **Susan Berry**, who developed the book with me; for her belief in the project, her perception of my working methods and the continuing dialogue on all matters concerning flowers, art, life and the universe; **Hilary Jagger**, for roses and projects; **Debbie Mole**, for designing a book that enhances my work; and **John Heseltine**, for faithful and inspirational photography. As always, they were all a pleasure to work with.